Stumbling Down the Road Less Traveled

A DEVOTIONAL: INSIGHTS INTO LIFE'S MISHAPS ON THE ROAD
- RECALCULATING EDITION

TONYA KAY MCKINLEY

AT THE WELL PRESS

Copyright © 2025 by Tonya Kay McKinley

All rights reserved.

No portion of this book may be reproduced in any form without written permission from the publisher or author, except as permitted by U.S. copyright law.

Scripture quotations marked (NLT) are taken from the Holy Bible, New Living Translation, copyright ©1996, 2004, 2015 by Tyndale House Foundation. Used by permission of Tyndale House Publishers, Carol Stream, Illinois 60188. All rights reserved.

Scripture quotations marked MSG are taken from The Message, copyright © 1993, 2002, 2018 by Eugene H. Peterson. Used by permission of NavPress. All rights reserved. Represented by Tyndale House Publishers.

Scripture quotations taken from the Amplified® Bible (AMP), Copyright © 2015 by The Lockman Foundation. Used by permission. lockman.orgScripture quotations taken from the Amplified® Bible (AMPC),Copyright © 1954, 1958, 1962, 1964, 1965, 1987 by The Lockman Foundation
Used by permission. lockman.org

Scripture quotations taken from the (NASB®) New American Standard Bible®, Copyright © 1960, 1971, 1977, 1995, 2020 by The Lockman Foundation. Used by permission. All rights reserved. lockman.org

Scripture quotations taken from The Holy Bible, New International Version®, NIV®. Copyright © 1973, 1978, 1984, 2011 by Biblica, Inc. Used with permission of Zondervan. All rights reserved worldwide. www.zondervan.com

Contents

Introduction	1
1. Peeping Toms?	3
2. A Hand to Hold	9
3. Meant to Be	15
4. Taxi, Please	19
5. In the Garden	25
6. Mona Lisa Smirks	33
7. Wake-Up Call	39
8. A Place to Lay My Head	47
9. Lost and Confused	53
10. Adventures, Prayers, Praise and Jumper Cables	60
11. A Perfect Moment	67

12. Americans: We ain't so Bad 73
13. Grounded 79
14. Here We Go Again 85
15. My Miracle on the Mountain 92
16. A Coastal Escapade: When Birds Attack (Sort of) ... 98
17. Midnight Snack 103
18. God, I Know You Can Move Mountains, But Can You Help Me Get Down One? ... 107
19. The What's Broke? 113
20. The Honeymoon Reef 117
21. Horsing Around 122
22. Dônde está el baño? (Where is the Bathroom?) ... 127
23. What's that Smell? 131
24. Rest of the Story 136
25. Just One Coffee 140
26. When the Journey Leaves a Mark 145
27. Lost and Found 149
28. Island Odyssey: A Golf Cart Adventure 152
29. Traveling Light 156
30. Fill'er Up 160

31.	When Silence Speaks	164
32.	The Sweetest Vacation	168
33.	Stow Aways	174
34.	The Road to Colorado	180
35.	When Autocorrect Gets Spiritual	185
36.	Enjoying the Pura Vida in Costa Rica	189
37.	Grief, Fur, and a New Beginning	194
38.	The Road to Rushmore: A Healing Trip West	199
39.	Waves of Grief, Currents of Grace	203
40.	The People Who Shape Us	208
Receive Jesus as Your Savior		215
About the Author		218

Introduction

SOMEDAY

In my heart, I have loved, traveled the nations, sought adventures, and found them. In my heart, I have dreamed impossible dreams and known passion and pain. In my heart, I know no fear and am not afraid of the heartbreaks that follow. Someday, I will catch up with my heart.

Tonya Kay McKinley

Life Insight: Catching Up

I wrote the poem "Someday" years ago, long before the travel and episodes you will read in the following pages. I was tired of dreaming, wishing, and staying nice and safe in my room. I wanted to see the world, experience life, taste new cultures, and fall in love. And that is just what I did.

I encourage everyone to find the strength to step out of their comfort zone and follow a dream or two. The Lord wants us to live an abundant life, so he came.

"I have come to give you life and life more abundantly." John 10:10, paraphrased

Too many people believe that God wants us to sit at home and live mediocre lives, but no, he never wanted that for us. He said, *"I want to give you the desires of your heart."* Psalm 37:4, paraphrased

Now, that does not mean we will not hit a few pitfalls along the way or ever experience heartbreak, but he said *"he would never leave us nor forsake us."* Hebrews 13:5, paraphrased

and no matter what happens, *"joy comes in the morning."* Psalm 30:5, paraphrased

I let life pass me by for too many years, but now I am catching up with my heart. Catch up with yours, too.

CHAPTER ONE

Peeping Toms?

Melanie—my cousin, best friend, and partner-in-crime—and I have always had a thing for spontaneous road trips. The kind where you toss a bag in the backseat, roll down the windows, and see where the day takes you. One chilly Saturday in December, we did just that.

I had been toying with the idea of transferring to a college tucked away in the North Carolina mountains, so we decided to scout it out. No formal tour, no appointment—just the two of us planning to blend in and explore. We packed up my tiny Geo Storm and hit the road for what we naively dubbed a "three-hour tour." (Cue *Gilligan's Island* theme.)

After about three hours winding through the highways from High Point, we arrived in Mars Hill—a quaint little college nestled in the Blue Ridge Mountains. The campus had that perfect small-town charm: small enough to feel like family, big enough to have a football team. I loved it. (Spoiler alert: I never did transfer—but that is beside the point. The real adventure came after we left.)

After exploring for about an hour, we figured, *Why waste the day?* So we set out for a scenic drive on the legendary Blue Ridge Parkway. Now, I had been a passenger along that route many times—but this was my first time driving those winding mountain roads myself. Let me tell you—while the views were breathtaking, so was my grip on the steering wheel.

The tiny guardrail separating us from the endless drop into the valley below was doing *nothing* to calm my nineteen-year-old nerves. Every time Melanie gasped and pointed out some distant beauty—"Wow! Look at that!"—my heart would skip a beat. Finally, I pleaded, "Melanie, please—just admire it quietly so I can focus!"

Still, the scene was unforgettable. Ice hung like crystal chandeliers from the rocky cliffs. The air was crisp, pure, and invigorating. We had always visited the Parkway in fall or spring, but that icy winter wonderland felt like stepping into Narnia. Well—Narnia with slightly higher stakes and a very inexperienced driver.

Then came Mount Mitchell—the highest point in the Blue Ridge. Out of nowhere, a thick fog descended like a wool blanket. I could barely see a few feet ahead. Knowing we were hugging a mountain edge, I slowed to five miles per hour, white-knuckled and praying under my breath.

"Pray, Melanie—and no talking!" I finally said, because nervous chatter was the last thing I needed. The tension in my shoulders was unreal. The whole world seemed eerily silent. No cars, no sounds—just us creeping through the fog like extras in a *Twilight Zone* episode.

When we finally emerged from that misty mountain, civilization reappeared. Other drivers were smart enough to avoid the summit that day. But now a new crisis hit: we were *desperate* for a restroom.

After hours in the car, our eyes were practically floating. But every restroom we passed was closed for the season. The Parkway does not close in winter unless absolutely necessary—but it seems the Parks Department closes every single restroom just to discourage people like us from wandering around.

No map. No plan. No shoulder to pull over on. We were trapped between a sheer rock wall and a cliff. No bushes. No options.

Finally, we spotted a potential rest area—a deserted restaurant with a parking lot. We rushed in—locked. But next to the building, stairs were carved into the mountainside, leading to a lower-level restroom. We sprinted down—locked again.

We were beyond desperate. "There is a rainwater drain here," I suggested. Melanie, equally desperate, said, "Good enough. I will stand guard."

I handled my business quickly. But just as it was Melanie's turn, a car pulled in. Out came a couple and their dog—heading straight for us.

"Hurry, Melanie! Someone is coming!" I whispered.

"I cannot hurry—I have been holding it too long!" she hissed, mid-squat.

I was laughing so hard I almost had to go again. Melanie was trying not to get caught with her pants down—literally. And just when we thought the situation could not get more ridiculous, we glanced up ... and saw two guys on a ridge above us, watching with binoculars!

When they realized they were busted, they gave us a cheerful wave. We burst out laughing, waved back, and sprinted to the car—two giggling girls with a story no one would believe.

Life Insight: Stumbling Blocks

Sometimes life reminds us—*you never know who is watching*. That day, it was a couple hikers with binoculars. But every day, as believers, the world is watching us too.

It may not seem fair, but people are paying attention. They are watching to see if your walk matches your talk—especially when you face difficulty, frustration, or even a ridiculous moment on a road trip.

The Apostle Peter puts it this way:

> *Dear friends, I warn you as "temporary residents and foreigners" to keep away from worldly desires that wage war against your very souls. Be careful to live properly among*

your unbelieving neighbors. Then even if they accuse you of wrongdoing, they will see your honorable behavior and they will give honor to God when he judges the world.

1 Peter 2:11-12, NLT

That is what we are called to—living in such a way that even our mistakes and stumbles reflect the grace and goodness of God.

Jesus said it this way:

"In the same way, let your good deeds shine out for all to see so that everyone will praise your heavenly Father."

NIV

But oh, how often we blend right in with the world—watching the same movies, excusing the same behaviors, dressing like everyone else. Then we wonder why some accuse the church of hypocrisy.

We are called to be **set apart**. A chosen generation. A royal priesthood. A holy nation. It is time to start living like it.

Will we fail? Of course. We are human. But God's mercies are new every morning. When we stumble, we get back up. We repent. We live with grace and humility, so the world sees not perfection—but a Savior who loves and transforms imperfect people.

And next time you find yourself in a crazy moment on a mountain road—remember: **Someone is always watching.** Let them see Jesus in how you handle even the most ridiculous situations.

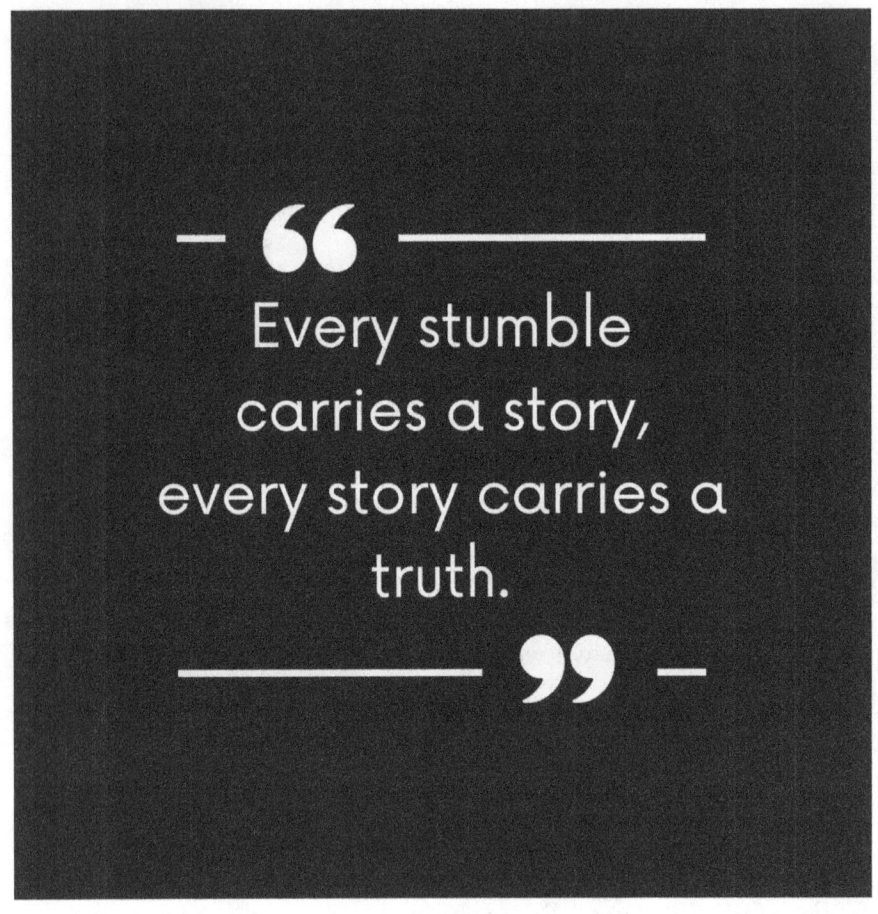

Chapter Two
A Hand to Hold

It was just two weeks before Thanksgiving, and life had thrown me into a whirlwind. The bank I worked for had recently acquired another bank in West Virginia, and I was selected to join the merger team. Our mission was to help the newly acquired branches transition smoothly, which meant spending a few weeks on-site in unfamiliar territory. I was flying out of Greensboro, North Carolina, with a layover in Pittsburgh, Pennsylvania, before finally heading to Morgantown, West Virginia. I had flown plenty of times before, but this trip was about to be one for the books.

After a routine layover in Pittsburgh, we boarded a much smaller plane for the final leg of the journey to Morgantown. I mean small: a mere sixteen seats, with a single row on each side and a narrow aisle in between. It was the kind of plane where you could feel every movement, and there was not even a flight attendant. Instead, the co-pilot took on double duty, checking our seatbelts and making sure the overhead compartments were secured. It was definitely a different experience, and I was already feeling a bit out of my element.

One of the most surprising things was the lack of a cockpit door. We could see straight out of the pilot's windshield—a rare sight for sure, and definitely something you wouldn't find on planes today (this was before 9/11, after all). They could have pulled a curtain to block the view, but they didn't bother. And honestly, part of me wishes they had, because the view out of that windshield on this particular flight was anything but reassuring. We were headed straight over the mountains on a cold, icy day. There was snow everywhere, and we had to wait for the wings to de-ice before we could even take off.

I'm no stranger to snow, but what I'd seen in North Carolina was nothing compared to the wintry conditions in West Virginia and Pennsylvania. I grew up on the coast of Texas, where snow is a rare novelty, so this was a whole new ballgame for me. Naturally, I was already a little on edge. Then the flight began, and let me tell you, it was an experience I'll never forget. The clouds were thick, and as I looked ahead at the mountains, it felt like we weren't flying all that high above them. But the real challenge came with the turbulence.

Oh, the turbulence. I've flown many times, but this was on another level. We'd be cruising along, and then suddenly, we'd hit a patch of rough air that sent the plane bouncing. The bumps were terrible enough, but it got worse as we neared Morgantown. The turbulence became more intense, and now, instead of just bumping around, we'd hit a pocket of air and drop—plummeting for what felt like a terrifying eternity. It was like being on a roller coaster but with none of the fun and all of the fear. And unlike a roller coaster, no tracks kept us steady. For the first time in my life, I started to feel airsick, and I don't think I'd ever been so scared. The flight was only thirty minutes long, but it felt like it stretched forever.

What happened when we finally landed, though, is something I'll never forget. As the plane came to a stop, I suddenly realized that the woman sitting next to me and I was holding hands—clinging to each other for dear life. Neither of us had even noticed we'd reached out for comfort during the flight; it was just something that happened instinctively, in a moment of shared fear and vulnerability. We looked at our hands, then at each other, and burst out laughing—a mix of relief and the realization of what we'd just been through together. We found solace in each other in that moment of need, and I was so grateful she was there.

After that ordeal, I made it home for Thanksgiving, but the respite was short-lived. I soon found out I had to return to West Virginia for another week. This time, though, I wasn't about to get back on that tiny plane. Instead, I opted to fly into Pittsburgh and rent a car to drive the rest of the way to West Virginia. The drive was much more peaceful, and I was able to enjoy the beautiful, snow-covered scenery without feeling like my life was hanging in the balance. It was a decision I definitely didn't regret—much better than the roller coaster ride.

Life Insight: Encouragement

God calls us to be encouragers, uplift, and strengthen one another in our faith journey. The apostle Paul reminds us in 1 Thessalonians 5:11,

> "Therefore encourage (admonish, exhort) one another and edify (strengthen and build up) one another, just as you are doing."
>
> TAB

This verse captures what it means to be part of the body of Christ—an interconnected community where each member plays a vital role in supporting the others.

When we see a friend or loved one in need, it's not just an opportunity; it's a divine calling to step in and be a source of strength and encouragement. Our love for Jesus should propel us into action, reflecting the selfless love He demonstrated for us. As Jesus Himself teaches in Matthew 25:40,

> "Inasmuch as ye have done it unto one of the least of these my brethren, ye have done it unto me."
>
> KJV

This powerful statement reminds us that every act of kindness, no matter how small, is an act of service to our Lord. When we serve others, we serve Christ, tangibly embodying His love and compassion.

Mother Teresa of Calcutta, India, captured this truth beautifully: "Because I cannot see Christ, I cannot express my love to Him in person. But my neighbors, I can see, and I can do for them what I would love to do for Jesus if He were visible. We are His co-workers—a fruit-bearing branch of His vine." Her words are a profound reminder that our love for God is best expressed through our love for others. We are called to be His hands and feet, to be the branches that bear the fruit of His love in the lives of those around us. This is a truth we should keep close to our hearts, allowing it to guide our daily actions and attitudes.

One of the most potent examples of this kind of love and dedication is found in the story of the four friends who carried their paralyzed friend to Jesus. This story, recounted in Mark 2:3-5 and Luke 5:18-20, illustrates the lengths we should be willing to go to help those in need. These four men faced a daunting challenge—their friend could not walk, a thick crowd surrounded the only one who could heal him, and there was no way to reach Him. Yet, they did not let this obstacle stop them.

Instead of giving up, they came up with a bold plan. They carried their friend onto the roof of the house where Jesus was teaching, and then they tore through the roof to lower him down to the feet of the

Savior. This was no small task. It required determination, creativity, and a willingness to get their hands dirty. But their love for their friend and their faith in Jesus drove them to take on the challenge. Their actions speak volumes about the commitment and devotion we are called to have for those we care about.

These men exemplify what it means to be true friends—friends willing to do whatever it takes to help and encourage those in need. They didn't let the first sign of difficulty deter them. They didn't let the hard work or the obstacles in their path discourage them. They were determined to see their friend healed and willing to tear through roofs to make it happen. This story challenges us to examine our lives and ask ourselves if we are willing to go the extra mile for others with the same kind of conviction and faith.

We, too, are called to be like these four friends, to help those in need with the same level of faith, dedication, and determination. It may not always require tearing off roofs—sometimes, all it takes is a simple act of kindness. But whatever the need, we are called to be champions for those who cannot help themselves. Let us be the kind of friends willing to go above and beyond, ready to do whatever it takes to bring others to the feet of Jesus, where true healing and restoration can be found. It may not even take tearing off roofs; all it may take is a hand to hold.

Chapter Three

Meant to Be

The summer of 1997 would be life-changing—I was spending it in Mexico as a missionary. While I was beyond excited, the months leading up to my departure were a whirlwind of preparation. I had to arrange for a leave of absence from work, ensuring my bills would be covered for the two and a half months I'd be gone. I also had to secure flights—first to Chicago for two weeks of training and then to Mexico—while juggling countless other expenses and tasks.

I worked as a teller at a local bank, and my coworkers and family were incredibly supportive. My cousin Melanie even offered to help with my car note, and friends and family gave generously to fund my trip. Despite these blessings, unexpected costs kept popping up, and I felt the strain. I knew this mission trip was God's plan, but staying positive wasn't always easy.

Two weeks before I was set to leave, it felt like everything was unraveling. I had just paid my six-month car insurance premium, which cost more than I expected. Then I had to buy my ticket to Chicago, which also turned out to be more expensive. By the end of that day, I was drained—emotionally, financially, and spiritually. That evening, the bank was hosting a 125th-anniversary celebration. I had zero interest in attending, but a coworker begged me to come so she wouldn't have to go alone. Reluctantly, I agreed.

The party was festive, with decorations, a buffet, and even line dancing. After we ate, a bank officer started announcing prizes for a drawing. There were TVs, VCRs, and restaurant gift cards—tons of great giveaways. I didn't win anything, and honestly, I was disappointed; there were so many at least I could have one something. But then they brought out the big-ticket items: three giant checks for $500, $1,000, and $1,500, plus a grand prize trip to Disney World with extra vacation time and spending money.

As the officer called out the winner for the $1,000 check, I was lost in thought, daydreaming about how helpful that money would be for my trip. Suddenly, my coworker started shaking my arm and screaming, "You won! You won!" It took me a moment to realize she was talking about me. I had won the $1,000 check!

When I walked up to claim the oversized check, I was stunned. This was more than a financial blessing—it was a heavenly reminder. God was reassuring me that this mission trip was meant to be. All the challenges and unexpected expenses couldn't overshadow His provision.

On the way home, I couldn't stop praising Him. This wasn't just a random win but a message from my loving Heavenly Father. And yes, my uncle teased me later, saying that next time, I should pray more specifically for the $1,500 check—I'll have to remember that.

Life Insight: He Meets Our Needs

> *"And my God will meet all your needs according to the riches of his glory in Christ Jesus."*
>
> Philippians 4:19, NIV

This verse powerfully reminds us of God's abundant provision and unwavering faithfulness. It speaks to more than just financial needs—it encompasses every area of our lives where we feel stretched, inadequate, or uncertain. God's resources are limitless, and He delights in providing for His children in practical and deeply personal ways.

In moments of doubt, like when I faced mounting expenses and growing frustration before my mission trip, it's easy to wonder if we're genuinely on the path God has called us to walk. But just as He did for me through the unexpected blessing of a $1,000 prize, God reassures us of His presence and plans. He may not always provide in the way we anticipate, but He always provides in the way we need.

This scripture also points to the source of all provision—His glory in Christ Jesus. The riches of His glory are not merely material; they include His grace, peace, joy, wisdom, and strength. God doesn't just meet our needs; He meets them in a way that reflects His love and reveals His glory in our lives.

When we trust God with our needs, we acknowledge He is our ultimate provider. He invites us to cast our cares on Him, not so we can passively wait for solutions but so we can step forward in faith, knowing He will make a way. Just as God aligned everything for my mission trip—through generous family, a supportive workplace, and even that check at the bank party—He orchestrates the details of our lives for His purposes.

As you meditate on this verse, consider the areas where you await God's provision. Are you trusting Him fully? Are you looking for His hand in the small details? Take heart in knowing that His timing and resources are sufficient. The same God who provided manna in the wilderness and calmed the stormy seas is the one who cares deeply about your every need.

Remember, when God calls you to something, He will equip you. You can move forward confidently, knowing that His provision is not just a promise—it's a guarantee rooted in His unchanging nature. Let this verse be a reminder to walk by faith, trusting that God will meet your needs according to the riches of His glory.

Whether it's financial support for a mission trip, peace in a challenging season, or strength to face a difficult day, God's provision is always on time and always enough. Trust Him and rest assured that He is faithful to meet you right where you are.

Chapter Four

Taxi, Please

In the summer of 1997, I had the incredible opportunity to work as a summer servant in Mexico. You might be wondering, *What exactly is a summer servant?* Great question. A summer servant was not a housekeeper or cook. Instead, it was a short-term missionary role, working alongside long-term missionaries to serve local communities and share the love of Christ.

The title "summer servant" sparked curiosity, even among the locals. I still chuckle thinking about a Mexican craftsman's confusion when he was commissioned to create our farewell gifts—a hand-painted plate featuring the town's name with "Summer Servant 1997" written in Spanish along the bottom edge. Perplexed, he asked why we Americans only had servants in the summer. His genuine bewilderment gave us all a good laugh.

There were five of us summer servants that year, engaged in friendship evangelism. Our days were filled with teaching English classes, hosting kids' clubs, performing mime acts in the town square, and organizing coffee houses. Each activity created opportunities to share the gospel, and it was a summer overflowing with joy, learning, and connection. I made lifelong friends, gained a deeper understanding of my faith, and discovered more about Jesus and how to share His love with others.

Midway through the summer, the missionaries treated us to a weekend in Mexico City to immerse ourselves in the rich heritage and culture. We explored museums, pyramids, theaters, and markets and indulged in authentic Mexican cuisine (a personal favorite). One of the most memorable stops was the Basílica de Guadalupe, a stunning Catholic church housing the cloak of Juan Diego with the image of the Virgin Mary.

As I approached the Basílica, I noticed a young girl crawling on her knees across the grounds toward the church. It was a sobering sight. Her act of penance, covering nearly 200 feet, left me heartbroken. I wanted to take her aside and gently explain that Jesus had already paid the price for her sins. She didn't need to earn His grace—it was freely given. And yet, she wasn't alone. Many others were performing similar acts of devotion, each trying to prove their worthiness. It was both humbling and heartbreaking to witness.

Another highlight was visiting the Sun and Moon Pyramids in the valley of Teotihuacan, just outside Mexico City. The grandeur of the ancient ruins was awe-inspiring, even if our tour guide's explanations left much to be desired. He seemed to improvise his history lessons, once pointing to carvings of fish and declaring they proved the Mayans traded with coastal tribes. I couldn't help but wonder, *Couldn't they have been freshwater fish?* Despite the questionable commentary, climbing the Sun Pyramid was unforgettable.

At the summit, we stumbled upon a New Age group performing a ritual in a circle. One of my friends casually walked through the center, disrupting their ceremony. Looking back, it probably wasn't the most respectful thing to do, but it was hard to stay silent in the face of people worshiping a dead god.

But perhaps the taxi rides were the most thrilling—and terrifying—part of the trip. Navigating Mexico City, a metropolis of over 30 million people, was an adventure in itself. Traffic was so congested that drivers alternated days based on their license plate numbers. Cars weaved through lanes with little regard for painted lines or traffic signals.

At one point, our taxi sped through a red light without even slowing down. Alarmed, I asked, "Wasn't that a red light?" The driver shrugged nonchalantly and replied, "There wasn't a car coming." While technically true, there were plenty of cars nearby. By God's grace, none were in the intersection at that moment. After that, I closed my eyes and prayed. Who would've thought I'd learn a lesson about faith in the back of a Mexican taxi? The Lord truly works in mysterious ways.

That summer changed me. It taught me about faith, friendship, and the lengths Jesus went to so we could experience His love and grace. Even now, I look back on those weeks in Mexico with gratitude and awe, amazed at how God used every moment to shape my heart and deepen my trust in Him.

Life Insight: God's Grace is a Gift, Not a Wage

One of the most striking moments from that summer in Mexico is forever etched in my memory. We were visiting the Basílica de Guadalupe—a grand, iconic site filled with reverence and tradition. The place was bustling with pilgrims, candles flickering, prayers whispered, the air thick with devotion.

Then I saw her.

A young girl, no older than maybe ten or eleven, crawling on her knees along the hard stone path leading up to the church. Inch by inch, step by painful step, she moved forward—her tiny hands trembling, her knees raw and reddened against the rough ground.

Her devotion was undeniable. Her determination humbling. But my heart broke for her.

In her eyes, you could see the silent cry: *"I must earn His love. I must prove my worth. I must atone for my sins."*
And all I wanted to do was run to her, wrap her in my arms, and whisper: *"Sweet girl, you don't have to do this. Jesus already did it all for you."*

That image has never left me. It was such a powerful, heartbreaking reminder of how easy it is for any of us to fall into the trap of believing that we must somehow *earn* God's grace. That salvation is something to be bargained for, paid for, proved through suffering or works.

But here is the beautiful truth: Grace is a **gift**. Not a wage. Not a prize for good behavior. A gift.

Ephesians 2:8-9 says it with breathtaking clarity:

> *"For it is by grace you have been saved, through faith—and this is not from yourselves, it is the gift of God—not by works, so that no one can boast."*
>
> NIV

If salvation were dependent on what we could do—how perfectly we performed, how much we sacrificed—we would not stand a chance. No matter how sincere or devoted we are, our best efforts will always fall short of God's perfect standard.

That is why Jesus came. He lived the perfect life we never could. He bore the punishment we deserved. He rose again to offer us eternal life.

That young girl's devotion touched me deeply—but it also reminded me of my own tendencies. How often have I caught myself thinking, *If only I pray harder... If I serve more... If I just do this or that, maybe then I will feel closer to God. Maybe then I will be "worthy."*

But grace cannot be earned. It can only be **humbly received.**

That summer in Mexico taught me something profound about the heart of God: He does not want us to come crawling to Him in shame, burdened by guilt, trying to prove ourselves. He wants us to come as children—arms wide open, trusting, running to our Father who has already done everything necessary to bring us close.

It is not about what we have done. It is about what **He** has done. Not about what we can give, but about what **He** freely gives.

Honestly? I did not deserve to experience God's goodness and protection during my time in Mexico—or to survive a taxi ride through Mexico City, for that matter! And I do not deserve His forgiveness, love, or blessing any more today than I did then.

And yet... He gives them. Freely. Lavishly. Because of who He is—not because of anything I have done.

That is the scandalous, beautiful truth of grace. And it changes *everything*.

So if you find yourself today trying to "earn" what has already been given, hear this invitation:

Stop crawling. Start running. Your Father is waiting—not with judgment, but with open arms. That is grace. And it is more than enough.

Chapter Five

In the Garden

It was Labor Day weekend, and you guessed it—Melanie and I were off on another adventure. This time, we were headed for the Outer Banks of North Carolina. Three days of lighthouses, wild ponies, and all the water we could soak up—all on our usual shoestring budget because, well, we never seemed to have much money. But who needs money when you have a tank of gas, a camera, and a best friend who loves a good road trip as much as you do?

We rolled into Kitty Hawk very late that Friday night and checked into a local hostel. Being the frugal travelers we were, we opted for the group room to save a few bucks. The best part? No one else had booked it. We had the whole space to ourselves! We took that as a sign—this weekend was going to be *epic*.

Saturday was postcard-perfect. We wandered the coast, visited stunning lighthouses, and even had a picnic beside a corral of wild ponies—because, why not? My dad had even slipped us some extra cash before we left and told us to "splurge on one good dinner." So we did. It was one of those days where everything seemed to go right—the kind of day you wish you could bottle up and revisit when life gets tough.

Sunday morning, we were ready for more. First up: the Wright Brothers Memorial. We goofed around at the museum, snapped silly pictures, and tried (and failed) to walk the length of the first flight. Spoiler alert—it looks short... until you try to walk it. Next, we made our way to Roanoke Island and started exploring the Elizabethan Gardens.

Oh, the gardens. They were absolutely breathtaking. Melanie and I wandered for hours, soaking in the beauty, relaxing in a gazebo overlooking the sound, even climbing a massive tree like a couple of carefree kids.

Eventually, it was time to move on. That is when the trouble began.

I had taken only my car key and camera with me, leaving everything else locked in the car—purse, phone, food, everything. As we headed back to the parking lot, I had a sinking feeling.

"Melanie, do you have the car key?"

"No... why would I?"

"Well... I lost it."

"You *what*?"

"I lost it."

"Okay… what do we do?"

"I have no idea."

Cue the panic.

We checked with the ticket office. No one had turned it in. So we retraced every step—every rock, every tree, every flower bed. We prayed. We pleaded. We searched again. Nothing.

My heart was pounding. Dad usually handled this kind of thing. But he was six hours away. I was stuck, clueless, and sinking fast into full-blown panic.

Desperate, we went back to the office. This time, a young woman overheard our dilemma and kindly offered to call AAA on our behalf since she was a member. She stayed with us—**for two hours**—while we waited for a locksmith. On a holiday weekend. On a Sunday. Talk about an angel in disguise.

When the locksmith finally arrived, he was less than thrilled about the job. But at that point, I just needed a key. It took him another two hours to make one and program it. Then came the kicker: he only accepted cash.

Not only had he jacked up the price, but he refused to let me go to the ATM alone. He took my license and followed me to the bank.

Now here is where the miracle happened.

At that point in my life, I barely had anything in savings. But somehow—**miraculously**—I had $350 sitting in my account. I praised God all the way to the ATM. Without that money, I do not know what I would have done.

Was it stressful? Yes. Expensive? Absolutely. But it was also a moment where I clearly saw God's provision.

Later that night, while praying, I asked, "Lord, why didn't You just show me where the key was? It would have saved me so much time and money!"

In my mind's eye, I saw a little child picking up the key and walking away, their parents completely unaware. And I sensed the Lord say, *"How could I show you where it was when it was no longer there?"*

That was a lesson I will never forget. Sometimes God answers in ways we do not expect. Sometimes the miracle is not prevention—it is **provision**.

And yes—now I own a $300 car key. Not exactly the souvenir I had in mind, but one that reminds me that God always comes through.

Life Insight: El Shaddai

El Shaddai. What a name! It is not just a title—it is a promise.

If you walk with Him long enough, you will discover that truth again and again. I have.

The checkbook runs low… and somehow, the money arrives. The anxiety creeps in… and peace that surpasses understanding settles over your heart. The path ahead looks foggy… and suddenly, God opens a door where there was none. He is the God who provides—not just financially, but emotionally, spiritually, relationally. **He is enough. Always.**

I am reminded of when Moses stood before the burning bush and asked, "Who shall I say sent me?" And God responded, *"I AM."* (Exodus 3:14)

Those two little words say it all: *"I AM your provider. I AM your healer. I AM your peace. I AM your everything."*

And God still operates that way today.

Luke 6:38 paints the picture beautifully:

> *"Give, and it shall be given unto you; good measure, pressed down, and shaken together, and running over, shall men give unto your bosom. For with the same measure that ye mete withal it shall be measured to you again"*
> Luke 6:38, KJV

God does not just meet needs—He exceeds them. He pours out blessings to overflowing.

And in Malachi 3:10, He invites us to test Him:

> "Bring ye all the tithes into the storehouse, that there may be meat in mine house, and prove me now herewith, saith the Lord of hosts, if I will not open the windows of heaven, and pour you out a blessing, that there shall not be room enough to receive it"
>
> Malachi 3:10, KJV

I have tested Him. I have seen Him do it. Again and again.

And do not forget Philippians 4:19:

> "And my God will meet all your needs according to the riches of His glory in Christ Jesus."
>
> NIV

All your needs—not just the ones you think are "spiritual" enough. Every single one.

Psalm 23:1 sums it up best:

> "The Lord is my shepherd; I lack nothing."
>
> NIV

When you walk with El Shaddai, you walk with the One who is more than enough. You are never alone. You are never without hope. So take Him at His Word. Trust Him. Watch Him prove Himself faithful—sometimes through a lost key, sometimes through unexpected provision, always through His boundless love. What an awesome God we serve!

Chapter Six
Mona Lisa Smirks

We had twelve whirlwind days to conquer Europe, which naturally meant devoting a full day to Paris. Can you see *all* of Paris in a day? Not really—but that did not stop us from trying!

By the time evening rolled around, I was running on fumes. Our final stop of the day? The Louvre. We thought we were being oh-so-smart by saving it for last, taking advantage of the discounted evening admission. Spoiler alert: Big mistake. Walking miles and miles through one of the world's largest museums *after* a full day of sightseeing? Let's just say this is not a strategy I recommend.

Mistake number two: not grabbing a map. "A map? For a museum?" I had scoffed. Oh, silly me. I figured we would breeze in, see the Mona Lisa, wander a bit, and head out victorious. Mistake number three: Never, I repeat *never*, "wander" in the Louvre. You might as well leave breadcrumbs or notify next of kin. That place is a maze of epic proportions.

At first, everything went according to plan. Signs for the Mona Lisa were everywhere—we followed them like Dorothy following the yellow brick road. Along the way, we marveled at the art, soaking in centuries of creativity.

Then, there she was—the Mona Lisa. I had imagined this moment for years. I had even rewatched *Ever After* before the trip, hoping to channel some da Vinci-inspired awe. I squeezed through the sea of tourists and finally stood face to face with her... and well... let's just say the buildup was better than the reality. It looked exactly like every replica I had ever seen—only smaller.

A little underwhelmed but still determined to enjoy the museum, we pressed on. That is when the real adventure began. One hallway turned into another, then another—and soon we realized: we were lost. Truly lost.

To make matters worse, I was starving. My last meal had been half a sandwich at the Eiffel Tower (the other half had been snatched by some overzealous birds). Now, lost and hangry, all I wanted was to find the exit.

Unfortunately, no one could agree on which direction to go. We asked a guard for help, but in the confusion, we lost track of Chad, who had wandered off on his own. Now it was just me, Kermit, and a vague set of directions from the guard.

We tried one hallway—dead end. Backtracked. Another hallway—back in the African art section. Not exactly where we wanted to be after several exhausting hours. Even stumbling upon the Venus de Milo did little to lift my spirits. I was *done*.

Then, a glimmer of hope: another "Mona Lisa this way" sign. I figured if I could just get back to her, maybe I could remember the way out. Sure enough, we made it back—and I am pretty sure the Mona Lisa was smirking at us this time.

Eventually, after much wandering and more than a few exasperated prayers, we found the pyramid entrance. And there stood Chad—grinning, perfectly relaxed. "What took you two so long?" he asked. Let's just say I resisted the urge to throttle him on the spot.

Life Insight: Consider It All Joy

Getting lost in a museum is one thing. Getting lost in life's trials? That is another matter entirely.

At some point, we all face seasons that feel disorienting—where every path seems like a dead end, and the way out feels impossible to find. It is in those moments that James 1:2-4 speaks so powerfully:

> "Consider it all joy, my brethren, when you encounter various trials, knowing that the testing of your faith produces endurance. And let endurance have its perfect

result, so that you may be perfect and complete, lacking in nothing"

NASB

We may not feel joyful when trials hit. In fact, we often feel lost, weary, and ready to give up. But here is the truth: God is working through those very challenges to build something lasting in us—endurance, patience, and a deeper faith.

Patience is not something that happens overnight. Just ask Abraham. He waited twenty-five long years before holding the son God had promised. Imagine the joy he must have felt when that promise finally came to life (Genesis 21:1-8).

Or Joseph—sold into slavery, wrongfully imprisoned, seemingly forgotten. Yet he clung to God's Word, believing the dreams God had given him. Years later, he rose to power in Egypt and watched those dreams unfold in ways he never could have imagined (Genesis 37-50).

Patience builds faith. Trials build endurance. And both are necessary if we want to see God's promises come to life.

One important note: **God does not test us with evil**. James 1:13 makes that clear:

> "Let no one say when he is tempted, I am being tempted by God; for God cannot be tempted by evil, and He Himself does not tempt anyone."

NASB

God's role is not to trip us up—it is to redeem and restore. He is the One who turns what the enemy meant for harm into something good. As James 1:17 reminds us:

> "Every good thing given and every perfect gift is from above, coming down from the Father of lights, with whom there is no variation or shifting shadow."
>
> NASB

So when life feels like an endless maze and you cannot see the way out, trust that God is working. He is not lost—He knows exactly where you are. And if you let Him, He will use this season to grow you, strengthen you, and lead you exactly where you need to be.

In the end, the trial you thought might undo you could very well become the very testimony that builds your faith—and encourages someone else along the way.

And who knows? You might even find yourself smiling at the lessons learned—you might find that a dream or two comes true along the way.

Chapter Seven

Wake-Up Call

It was my first night in Rang, a little village in the beautiful mountains of Haiti. The mission we were staying at was very primitive, with no electricity or plumbing. This place was definitely not for the faint of heart. That night, I went to my room to turn in. We still had the generator going, so I was trying to hurry and get into bed before they turned it off for the night. My room had a bed, and only my pack was in the corner. Did I mention there was no ceiling, just a high-pitched tin roof above, so you could hear everything going on in the house? The heat was so unbearable that I stripped down to just my underwear and did not even consider the shorts I brought to sleep in. Before crawling into my bed, I killed a spider the size of my palm, brushed the tiny ants off the sheets, and noticed a mouse crawling in the rafters above my head. Oh yes, there is nothing like sleeping in a third-world country. As I tried to get comfortable, the generator went out, and it then became pitch dark. I had never seen darkness like this before, nor have I ever heard the silence like this. No streetlights were in the windows, and no traffic, horns, or trains. Actually, I guess it was not as quiet as I thought. I heard a couple of crazy Haitian roosters, whose internal clocks were obviously off, and some dogs fighting in the yard that were about to drive me nuts, but the only other sounds were the sounds going on around the house. I saw a flashlight come on and heard someone yell, "Where is my pot to pee in?" and everyone burst out laughing. I found out a little earlier that they lock us into the house at night (for our own safety) and provide us with a chamber pot for the night. In my wildest dreams, I never thought I would ever be in a situation where I could use a chamber pot, but it was no worse than the outhouse we used during the day. Finally, people had settled in for the night because all was quiet. I had not been able to fall asleep yet, but I sure wish I had before the orchestra started: the tuba was across the hall, the trumpet next door, and it sounded like the brass section was down the hall—no ceilings made for great acoustics for the snore band. I should have packed the earplugs. Eventually, I must have fallen asleep from pure exhaustion.

Earlier that day, we woke up early in Port-au-Prince to head to the airport to catch the single-engine plane to Pignon. The plane could only carry one thousand pounds, so we had to split up our group. Darlene, I, and a young Haitian man we had just met named Senora were the first three to go. We flew over the mountains and landed on a grass airstrip thirty minutes later. The pilot pulled our bags out for us, then jumped back in the plane, turned around, and flew off, and I realized that this was it. There was no airport, no waiting room to sit in, just a shade tree in the middle of God knows where, with a Haitian who barely spoke English, Darlene, and me, who spoke no Creole. I did have three years of high school Spanish (the little I remembered) that helped some since Senora knew Spanish from working in the Dominican Republic. A truck drove up with five Haitian men. Darlene and I looked at one another, a little anxious. We did not know these men and were unsure what to expect. Being in Haiti for the first time, we hoped they were friendly and not there to harm or rob us. The men spoke to Senora and then offered to let us sit in the back of their truck. I didn't understand until about two hours later that they were our ride to the mission. We had to wait two-and-a-half hours for the other half of our group in the Haitian heat with half a bottle of water I just happened to have in my pack.

When our group finally arrived, we piled our bags, the five of us and seven or eight Haitians, into a tiny Toyota pickup truck, and off we went. I discovered that this is the Haitian way—everyone who can pile in or hang on in some way gets on the vehicle, and off they go. It makes for an exciting and very cramped ride. Another thing I learned is that it takes hours to go a few miles in Haiti. The roads are horrible; the rainy season cuts huge crevices into the roads. I don't think an excellent four-wheel drive vehicle would work—you need a tank to travel those roads. My tail end was killing me after half an hour, and we still had at least another hour left. I was sunburned and hot, and now we were broken down on the side of the road. The truck dropped its drive shaft. But no worries: these resilient Haitians somehow fixed it on the road, and off we went again. When we got to the river with no bridge, we tried to cross but couldn't make it up the hill on the other side. Everyone unloaded, which was difficult when there was no bumper because the four-wheel drive vehicle was pretty high off the ground. Poor Darlene fell off the truck, hind-end first (at least she landed on padding). We started climbing the hill while the men pushed the truck straight up. A young boy offered me his bike, and after riding in that cramped truck for hours, that sounded like a great idea. Our guide told me the mission was not too far ahead and that I couldn't miss it. Well, I did. I just rode right past it. Suddenly, I had little kids chasing me and yelling at me. I realized I must have passed it, so I started to turn around, but not before I came up to two men carrying machetes. Of course, they didn't mean any harm, but I, the only white girl in this God-forsaken country, an idiot who left her friends behind, was letting her imagination get the best of her. Oh please, God, don't let me die on my first day here, I prayed. I turned around, acted like I knew where I was going, and followed the children. I arrived at the mission with everyone laughing at me for passing it up and just ignored my heart pounding in my chest from my little vision of being hacked up by the machete-carrying Haitians. I asked to wash up as I was filthy from the trip. Dumb me, I wore white pants that morning, thinking how much cooler they would be in the heat, but those pants were now the color of the Haitian roads. This was just the first day of our adventure.

So there I was, finally asleep. Huh? What was that? It was still pitch black, and I heard screaming. Someone was coming up the road yelling and screaming. This is it, I figured; they are coming to kill the Americans. The man crying and screaming was trying to raise a posse to go and get us. It was getting closer.

"Donna," I whispered loudly. "Donna, are you awake?" Donna and Darlene were in the room next to mine.

"Yeah," she answered back.

"What in the world is that?" I asked.

"I have no idea," she answered.

"What do we do?" I asked her.

"I have no idea," she answered again, and I wondered, *"Is that all you have to say?"*

"What's Darlene doing?" I asked.

"She is sleeping," she answered, giggling now.

"Are you kidding me? Is she sleeping through this?" I couldn't help but giggle, too. I think this was the mental breakdown coming from the anxiety we were feeling before we were murdered in our beds.

"Donna, it's getting closer."

"I noticed."

"Pierre," I hear Brandon yell. "What in the world is that?"

We soon discovered that the man yelling down the road was the town crier calling the people to prayer at four o'clock in the morning. I was having a heart attack for nothing, so I turned over and went back to sleep, foregoing the morning prayer.

Life Insight: Made of Rubber

I have learned through the years that you must be flexible to win souls to Christ. This is especially true when you are dealing with people from another culture. It is so easy for us to become set in our ways, and, as Americans, we want it done now, and we want it done right. However, other cultures work differently. In my experience, most are laid back and not in any hurry, which irritates the snot out of us. If we let these things get to us, it can hinder the job God has for us. We have to learn to deal with it and get over these petty excuses if we want to be witnesses for Christ. Paul gives us some great advice in Philippians 4:11-13:

> "I have learned to be content whatever the circumstances. I know what it is to be in need, and I know what it is to have plenty. I have learned the secret of being content in any and every situation, whether well fed or hungry, whether living in plenty or in want. I can do everything through him who gives me strength."
>
> NIV

We have to learn to adapt if we want to evangelize the world. I know it is not easy here in the United States or abroad, but we have to be willing to bend and give, or we will snap in two.

Another bit of advice Paul leaves us is found in 1 Corinthians 9:20-23:

> "To the Jews I became like a Jew, to win the Jews. To those under the law I became like one under the law (though I myself am not under the law), so as to win those under the law. To those not having the law I became like one not having the law (though I am not free from God's law but am under Christ's law), so as to win those not having the law. To the weak I became weak, to win the weak. I have become all things to all men so that by all possible means I might save some."
>
> NIV

To witness to Japanese, you must become Japanese, and to witness to a Haitian, you must become Haitian, even if it means getting sunburned on a long, long drive along a bottom-busting road or getting a frightening wake-up call very early in the morning. Blessed are the flexible, for they shall not be broken (just a little bruised).

Chapter Eight
A Place to Lay My Head

We were in Saltillo, Mexico. It was my first mission trip, and I was thrilled and terrified. My Uncle Brandon, my cousins Micah and Jerry, and I made the long haul from North Carolina to Saltillo in two days. We were staying for a week, and let me tell you, I was ecstatic! I had always dreamed of going on a mission trip, but I had no idea what to expect. I hadn't been out of the country before, so this was a big deal.

Uncle Brandon was busy preaching sermons and doing electrical work for the mission. Meanwhile, I was doing... well, nothing. And I mean absolutely nothing. I was so disappointed in myself. I didn't know what to say or do, and to top it off, my Spanish was nonexistent. I was too nervous to talk to the congregation and even too shy to chat with the other youth group staying at the mission. By the middle of the week, I just wanted to go home. I felt like I was completely useless to God.

But then something changed. We went into the town, and I finally started understanding why we were there. As we drove around, I was shocked by what I saw. People were living in houses made of boards thrown together, wrapped in what looked like tinfoil and cardboard. Their drinking water was rainwater collected in fifty-gallon drums. I was stunned. Coming from my suburban home in the States, it was inconceivable that people could live this way. My heart was crushed. Then I realized why I was there: to receive Christ's heart and understand that Jesus weeps over His flock. I realized that the more His children know His heart, the more that will be done for those in need.

I returned home with a beautiful memory, though. On our last few days in Mexico, we headed to a small village in the mountains. And can you believe it? There was snow on the mountain caps in July! It was an incredible sight. The village itself was something else, too. There was no electricity, just an outhouse and animals wandering in and out of the house like they owned the place. Chickens and dogs would stroll in, making themselves at home.

The family we stayed with was excellent. They welcomed us with open arms and treated us like royalty. The woman of the house cooked us a delicious meal—lots of refried beans, which, let's say, I later regretted. Picture this: sharing a small room with two teenage boys who ate a huge pot of refried beans. It was a long, long night.

We had a wonderful service that evening, and afterward, we were supposed to sleep in the church. But the family wouldn't hear of it. They gave up their beds for us. I had never been so grateful. It had turned very cold that night, and we were unprepared. I had brought a sweatshirt and a light jacket, and I ended up lending the sweatshirt to Jerry and keeping the jacket for myself. We crammed into a bedroom with three beds; I had one to myself, and the guys had to share the others. But despite the cold, it was the warmest feeling I'd ever experienced. This wonderful family had nothing, yet they gave us everything they had—their warm beds, food to eat, and an abundance of generosity. It might have been a couple of feather blankets pinning me down that night, but their love kept me warm. And I will always be grateful for that.

Life Insight: Give All

My first mission trip taught me a lesson I'll never forget: Give what you have, and God will handle the rest. I left Mexico feeling pretty down like I hadn't made much of a difference. But when I looked back, God showed me so much more than I realized at the time.

It's a bit like the story in Mark when all these rich folks showed up at the temple, tossing large sums of money into the treasury. Then, a widow comes along and drops in two tiny coins, barely worth a penny. Jesus, of course, notices this and tells His disciples:

> "I tell you the truth, this poor widow has put more into the treasury than all the others. They gave out of their wealth; but she, out of her poverty, put in everything—all she had to live on."

Mark 12:43-44, NIV

She gave everything she had, and knowing God, I'm sure she was incredibly blessed. It reminds me of the story of the prophet Elijah when he meets a woman gathering sticks to make a final meal for herself and her son. Elijah asks her to make him a cake first, even though she's down to her last bit of flour and oil. She could've said, "Are you kidding me? This is all I've got!" But instead, she trusted God, made the cake, and guess what? Her jar of flour and jug of oil never ran dry. Talk about a miracle (1 Kings 17:11-13).

Then there's that famous story about a little boy with a small lunch—just a few loaves and fish. He didn't have much to offer, but he gave it to Jesus anyway. And what does Jesus do? He blesses it and turns that small lunch into a feast for thousands. (Matthew 14:13-21, Mark 6:30-44). Can you imagine? That little boy probably went home thinking, "Well, that was unexpected!"

The point is, never underestimate what you have to give. It might seem small to you, but it can turn into something huge in God's hands. The family in Mexico who gave us a warm bed and a meal—they didn't have much, but they gave generously, and they taught me what true generosity looks like. And while I might've felt like my time in Mexico didn't accomplish much that week, it planted a seed of love in my heart. That love has grown, encouraging me to minister to those in need. And who knows? Maybe that love will keep growing, touching lives worldwide, one little bit at a time.

So, remember, it's not about the size of the gift but the heart behind it. And when you give, God multiplies it in ways you might not see right away, but He's always at work, making something beautiful out of what we offer.

Chapter Nine
Lost and Confused

There we were—finally in the beautiful city of Amsterdam. This iconic city of canals would be the closest I would get to Venice on this trip, but that is a story for another time.

Amsterdam was on my dream list. I had so many sights I wanted to squeeze into our short stop: a houseboat or two, the homes and works of the city's famous painters, Anne Frank's house, and—yes—a quick peek at the infamous red-light district (strictly for curiosity's sake).

But first, we had to find our hostel. Sounds simple enough, right? Famous last words.

Although it was getting late, we thought we still had plenty of time to check in, stash our bags, and hit the town. We had an address. We had a very questionable map. We had confidence. Unfortunately, what we *did not* have was a clue.

We drove around for about forty minutes before finally stopping at a gas station to ask for directions. A kind gentleman gave us some new instructions, and we set off again—hope renewed. But Amsterdam is a very confusing city, especially to weary travelers. When you spot a sign, you had better double check if it is a road sign or a canal sign—or, better yet, a sign that makes no sense at all.

An hour passed. Then another. Now we had been circling for nearly three hours. I was in the backseat, watching the two men up front grow increasingly tense—one driving, one trying to decipher the map (and neither wanting to admit defeat). The charming streets of Amsterdam were quickly losing their magic.

As the lone female in the car, I kept offering what I thought was sage advice: *stop and ask someone else for directions*. This suggestion was ignored roughly every thirty seconds.

My secondary job became yelling up to the driver: "Watch out! Cyclist!"—because if there is one thing you learn quickly in Amsterdam, it is that cyclists rule the road. A distracted driver can easily take out a dozen bicycles in one blink.

At one point, I even suggested hiring a cab and simply following it to our destination. Brilliant idea, right? That one was also ignored.

Finally, we were stopped at a red light when inspiration struck—along with a hefty dose of frustration. I jumped out of the car (to the complete astonishment of my travel companions) and ran over to a man on a bicycle. "Excuse me, can you tell me how to get to this hostel?" I asked, breathless.

The cyclist smiled politely and said he only knew how to get there by bike—not by car. To this day, I am still trying to figure out exactly how that works. But at least I was trying!

At long last—after what felt like forty years wandering the wilderness (and I have a theory about that, by the way: the Israelites were led by a man)—I spotted the road sign. Yes, *I* found it. The lone female in the group, who was supposedly directionally challenged, was the one who got us there. No bitterness here... okay, maybe just a little.

We checked in, dropped off our packs, and parked the car in a garage. Now came the big question: What sight would we try to see in our precious remaining time? The guys were still debating when I decided to take matters into my own hands. I started walking.

"I have always wanted to see Anne Frank's house," I called over my shoulder. "If you are coming with me, you better hurry." Word of advice: never mess with a woman scorned—or a woman still annoyed that no one would stop for directions.

In the end, I got to see the one sight I had dreamed of. Standing inside Anne Frank's house, thinking of her bravery and resilience, was both humbling and moving—an experience worth every bit of frustration that led up to it.

We passed by the red-light district, but by then I was too tired (and too wary) to explore it at night. A quick glance was enough. We did pass a Rasta bar, though—a small surprise amid the winding streets.

That night, we walked along the canals, their lights shimmering on the water, the buildings glowing softly. It is funny how beauty can reappear once you take a deep breath and let go of your frustration. Even the companions who had you ready to scream three hours earlier can become your favorite dinner partners—yes, even over Italian food in Amsterdam (but that is another story altogether).

Life Insight: Directions

One of the most important lessons I learned on my trip to Amsterdam was this: sometimes, you need to stop and ask for directions.

Life can feel a lot like wandering through unfamiliar streets—twisting canals, confusing signs, and paths that seem to lead anywhere but where you intended. Decisions come at us daily—some small, some life-altering—and it can be easy to lean on our own understanding. After all, who knows us better than we know ourselves, right?

Wrong.

Proverbs gently reminds us:

> *"lean not unto our own understanding, acknowledge him and he will direct our paths."*
>
> KJV

God knows the number of hairs on our heads. If He knows *that* level of detail, do you not think He knows which way you should go? His plan for us is not one of random turns or accidental detours—it is a plan marked by peace and purpose.

The trouble comes when we, stubborn travelers that we are, keep barreling down the wrong road—ignoring the signs, refusing to stop, too prideful or too busy to pull over and ask for directions. And then, when we land in a place we never intended to be, we wonder why life feels so hard or unfair.

Here is a simple truth: **you will always reap what you sow.**

Yes, God is merciful. Yes, He forgives. But consequences are part of this life. You may be forgiven for betraying your spouse, but your marriage may still break under the weight of that betrayal. You may be forgiven for a lie, but trust—once broken—takes time and effort to rebuild.

This is why we need to consult God's roadmap: His Word.

> *"'For I know the plans I have for you,' saith the Lord, 'thoughts of peace, and not of evil, to give you an expected end'"*
>
> Jeremiah 29:11, KJV

God's path is not a trapdoor to pain—it is a road paved with peace, grace, and an expected end. But we must follow *His* directions, not our own.

> *"Thy Word is a lamp unto my feet and light unto my path."*
>
> Psalm 119:105, KJV

Without the lamp of God's Word guiding us, we are walking blind in a dark world. The lamp does not show us the entire road at once—but it gives us enough light for the next step. One step of obedience at a time will lead us exactly where we need to go.

And remember this: the Word is not just words on a page. The Word is *Jesus Himself*.

> "*In the beginning was the Word, and the Word was with God, and the Word was God... In him was life; and the life was the light of men. And the light shineth in darkness; and the darkness comprehended it not.*"
>
> John 1:1, 4-5, KJV

The world stumbles in darkness because it does not recognize the Light. But we have the Light—our Savior, the Word made flesh. When we look to Him, lean on Him, and trust His Word, we will not wander aimlessly.

So today—whatever decision you are facing, whether it is a small choice or a life-defining one—pause and ask for directions. Open His Word. Listen for His voice. Let the Holy Spirit guide your steps.

You may not see the entire map, but the One who wrote it is holding your hand. And when He directs your path—you will never, ever be lost.

Chapter Ten
Adventures, Prayers, Praise and Jumper Cables

In the summer of 1996, Melanie and I came up with what we thought was the perfect plan: we'd take our two younger cousins, Ashly and Kristen, to Atlanta Fest. Held at Six Flags Over Georgia, Atlanta Fest was a four-day extravaganza of Christian concerts featuring some of our favorite artists. The cherry on top? We'd be camping out in tents for the entire event—a combination of adventure, music, and family bonding.

We convinced Ashly's parents to fly her from Texas to North Carolina. Then, on a Wednesday morning, the four of us—Melanie, Ashly, Kristen, and me—packed into my recently acquired Ford Explorer for the drive to Atlanta. I loved that truck. It was an XLT model, complete with leather seats and all the bells and whistles, and it looked sharp. We piled our tents, luggage, and what felt like half a department store onto the roof rack and into the back. By the time we were packed, the truck was so loaded you'd think we were embarking on a summer-long expedition instead of a five-day trip.

The drive started smoothly, but as luck would have it, we hit road construction and found ourselves idling in the heat. That's when the dreaded "check engine" light flickered on. Panic started to creep in, but I rolled down the windows and turned off the air conditioning. Miraculously, the light went off, so we braved the sweltering heat until traffic started moving again. It wasn't pleasant, but in hindsight, it felt like a warm-up for the blazing temperatures we'd endure while camping.

Seven hours later, we arrived in Atlanta and secured a camping spot in a makeshift campground set up in a back parking lot of Six Flags. The site had temporary shower stalls and port-a-potties—a far cry from luxury but perfect for the adventure we had in mind. We claimed a spot between a camper and another tent and spent the next hour setting up camp. Melanie and I planned to share a four-person tent while Ashly and Kristen stayed in a smaller two-person one. Naturally, the girls refused to sleep alone, so the four of us crammed into the larger tent while our clothes and gear were relegated to the smaller one.

The week was brutally hot, with temperatures in the nineties. By Friday, we decided to take a break from the concerts and explore downtown Atlanta. We parked at a MARTA station and rode the train into the city, which was a new and exciting experience for the girls. Downtown, we packed in as much as we could. We toured the Coca-Cola Museum, shopped in Underground Atlanta, and had lunch at Planet Hollywood. Afterward, we spent hours at Coca-Cola's Olympic City, an eight-acre plaza filled with virtual reality attractions in honor of the upcoming Summer Olympics. We raced against a virtual Jackie Joyner-Kersee (guess who won!), balanced on a low beam, and competed on an obstacle course. It was a day of non-stop fun, and by the time we got back to the MARTA station, we were completely wiped out.

But the day's adventure wasn't over. When I turned the key in the Explorer's ignition, nothing happened. A second attempt yielded the same result. Exhausted and a little nervous, I suggested we pray. Together, we asked God for help. When we said "Amen," I turned the key again—and the engine roared to life. We cheered and thanked God for answering our prayer, feeling a renewed sense of His presence and care. That night, we made it back in time for Michael W. Smith's concert, the perfect finale to an amazing day.

Despite our fun, the relentless heat and the girl's dwindling funds convinced us to cut the trip short by a day. On Saturday morning, we packed up our campsite and loaded the truck. But when I tried to start the Explorer, it wouldn't budge. We prayed again,

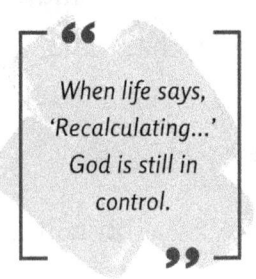

When life says, 'Recalculating...' God is still in control.

but this time, the answer came in the form of a kind neighbor who helped jump-start the truck. Ironically, he was driving an old, beat-up VW van, and seeing him reviving my high-dollar SUV was enough to make us all laugh. It was a fitting end to a trip full of unexpected moments and reminders of God's provision.

Looking back, that week was unforgettable—not just for the music and memories but also for the lessons in faith, flexibility, and finding joy in the journey.

Life Insight: Trusting God in the Unexpected

Life is full of detours, delays, and surprises—those moments that sneak up on us, test our patience, and stretch our faith. No matter how carefully we plan, life has a way of reminding us that we are not in control.

Take that trip to Atlanta Fest, for example. We faced our fair share of unexpected challenges: an engine light that stubbornly came on, sweltering heat, and a truck that decided it just was not interested in starting. At every turn, we had a choice—give in to worry or turn our hearts toward God.

And here is what I learned: **every single time we prayed, God showed up**. Sometimes the answer came quickly. Sometimes it came through the unexpected kindness of a stranger. But without fail, God met us in the middle of our need.

Those moments brought Proverbs 3:5-6 alive to me:

> *"Trust in the Lord with all your heart and lean not on your own understanding; in all your ways submit to him, and he will make your paths straight."*
>
> NIV

Now, trusting God does not mean life will always be smooth sailing. Far from it. But it does mean we do not have to navigate the bumps and detours alone.

It is easy to trust God when the road is clear and the journey is pleasant. But what about when the engine light comes on—literally or figuratively? What about when your plans fall apart, when the door you were hoping for slams shut, or when the waiting seems endless?

Those moments are not failures of faith—they are invitations. Invitations to lean in a little closer. To depend on Him more fully. To remember that His understanding far exceeds our own.

Sometimes God answers in a dramatic way—a miracle that leaves you speechless. Other times, His provision comes through a small kindness: a stranger who offers help, a friend who shows up just when you need them, an old VW van that gives your truck the jump-start it needs to get moving again.

But in every case, God is present. He is faithful. He is working—even when we cannot yet see the outcome.

So the next time life throws a curveball your way, pause and pray. Take a deep breath and invite God into the moment. Ask Him for wisdom, guidance, and peace. And trust that even if the solution is not immediate or what you expected, He is at work on your behalf.

Let life's challenges become opportunities to experience God's faithfulness in fresh, personal ways. And when the breakthrough comes—whether in a big or small way—pause to rejoice. Give thanks. Remember that the God who guided you through this unexpected moment will guide you through the next one, too.

And perhaps, like me, you will find that the detours become some of the most treasured parts of your journey—because they are where we learn to trust God most.

CHAPTER ELEVEN

A Perfect Moment

It was the week before Thanksgiving, and I found myself in Morgantown, West Virginia, knee-deep in one of the most challenging bank mergers of my career. The past week and a half had been long, draining, and emotionally exhausting. I was counting the days until I could go home and spend Thanksgiving with my family.

But that hope was short-lived. I had just received word that I would be returning to West Virginia again—this time the Sunday after Thanksgiving. I felt like the last little thread of my patience had just snapped.

To make matters worse, the merger itself was going downhill fast. Tensions were high. Employees were upset, and several key team members had resigned, leaving morale at an all-time low. I did everything I could to stay positive for the team, but inside, I was completely spent. My usual ability to keep my cool was slipping through my fingers.

By three o'clock that afternoon, I had not even had a chance to take a restroom break. I knew if I did not get out of that office soon, I would either break down or blow up—neither of which was an option.

So, I grabbed my coat and told everyone I would be back in about half an hour. I was not hungry. I was not going anywhere in particular. I just needed a moment to breathe, to clear my head, and to pray.

As soon as I walked out the door, I whispered, "Lord, I need peace. I am usually good at staying calm—that is why I am good at this job. But today? I cannot do it anymore. I am too tired."

Even after that simple prayer, I was too weary to say much more. So, I just kept walking.

At first, my mind was still spinning with stress, but then something shifted. I felt the Holy Spirit nudge me: *Look up. Look around.*

When I did, I noticed the beauty all around me. I was downtown, walking past old buildings dressed up for the holidays. Shop windows sparkled with Christmas decorations, and to my surprise—it was snowing.

Not just any snow. Big, fluffy, magical flakes were falling gently from the sky. I stopped in my tracks.

For a moment, I could not resist—I stuck out my tongue and caught a snowflake or two. The stress that had been weighing me down lifted just a bit. Suddenly, it felt like I had stepped into an old black-and-white movie. The cold air, the soft snow, my long black wool coat and matching hat—it was a scene straight out of *It's a Wonderful Life*.

No, I did not run down the street shouting, "I'm alive!" like George Bailey—but I did stop right there and thank God for that perfect, peaceful moment. His beauty broke through my exhaustion and reminded me that peace is always available—we just have to pursue it.

I returned to the office with a renewed spirit and a clear mind. The situation had not changed, but I had. And sometimes, that is the greater miracle.

Life Insight: Pursue Peace

Psalm 34:14 says it plainly:

> *"Depart from evil and do good; seek peace, and pursue it."*
>
> KJV

Notice that peace does not always come knocking on our door. Sometimes, we have to seek it. Pursue it. Go after it with intention—especially when life feels chaotic and heavy.

Storms will not always pass on their own. Deadlines will not disappear. Difficult people may still be difficult. But in the middle of it all, we can choose to pursue peace.

Philippians 4:7 promises:

> *"The peace of God, which passeth all understanding, shall keep your hearts and minds through Christ Jesus."*
>
> KJV

God's peace transcends understanding. It is not logical. It is not based on whether our circumstances change. It is based on the unchanging nature of *who He is*.

But here is the key: when we pray and ask God for peace, we must be willing to receive it. If we pray and then let worry take right back over, we are essentially telling God we do not trust Him to handle it.

I once heard a beautiful story about an art contest. Artists were asked to paint a scene that depicted *peace*. Many painted calm lakes, serene fields, snowy nights.

But the winning painting was quite different. It showed a raging storm—lightning, crashing waves, wind whipping through the air. And on a tiny branch, in the middle of it all, a small bird slept soundly, completely at peace.

That is the kind of peace God offers us. Not the absence of storms, but the presence of stillness in the middle of them.

Remember Mark 4:38-40—Jesus was asleep in a boat while a storm raged around Him. His disciples were terrified and woke Him up. Jesus calmed the storm with three simple words: *"Peace, be still."*

Then He asked them, *"Where is your faith?"*

Let me ask you the same question today: **Where is your faith?**

When life's storms rage, we must believe God's Word is true. We can speak to our storms and declare, *"Peace, be still."* And when we do, we can trust that His peace will guard our hearts and minds.

The next time you feel yourself spinning with stress or ready to snap—pause. Pray. Look around. Find His beauty. Pursue His peace.

And maybe—just maybe—stick out your tongue and catch a snowflake or two.

Chapter Twelve

Americans: We ain't so Bad

It was February 2003, and I had the opportunity to go to Europe to see a friend who was stationed in Germany. Everyone told me I was crazy to go because we were on the brink of war. I decided not to let this chance pass me by; besides, the flights were so cheap at the moment. So I packed my bags and left for a twelve-day whirlwind tour of Europe. I cannot say that I was not nervous about war or terrorism; even the base where my friend was stationed was on high alert. It was a little daunting to see a manned tank facing the front gate while we were there. However, my uncle decided to take the trip with me, which put me at ease. My mom was so much happier about my going now that my uncle was coming along.

What was funny is that once people found out we were Americans, they had to tell us what they thought about the war, America, or President Bush. There were war protests at several places we visited, and it got to the point where I was ready to start telling everyone I was Canadian. One woman on the Paris subway told me what she thought of President Bush and that "at least President Clinton was human." I couldn't help chuckling at the look on her face when I told her my opinion of Clinton and that I voted for Bush and planned on voting for him again.

I learned on this trip that I am proud to be an American. We are so blessed as a nation and a people, and too many times, we do not even realize it. The American people, on the whole, are warm and generous and willing to help. My fellow travelers and I proved it. We were on a train from Cologne, Germany, headed back to home base, and the train conductor was walking the aisle checking tickets. When the conductor came to the young man seated across from us, he did not have enough money for his fare. So my friends and I started digging in our pockets, ready to hand over what he needed. There were three of us, but our train ticket was good for four, so the conductor said we did not have to pay any money; he would use the fourth unused ticket on our pass. The young man nodded his thanks, and we just smiled and told him no problem.

At one point on the ride, we came to a town, and the conductor told us that this was the end of the line. We were a little confused because we were still a ways from home. He informed us that another train would come along in about an hour, but we had to get off this train. It was late Sunday night, and the small train station was closed, so we headed to the only open place: a colorful local bar. We were seated inside, ordered a drink, and checked out the scene. The place was packed. The young man who used our ticket was there with some

German soldiers and a group on the other side of the bar playing darts. We were there for a little while when the table next to us, the soldiers and our friend, struck up a friendly conversation. We had a good time, and we were back on the train before we knew it. The soldiers said goodbye, but our fourth passenger followed us back on the train. He and my uncle had started a deep conversation in the bar and continued it on the train. It was exciting to see how my uncle managed to turn the conversation over to Christ. I prayed for my uncle's direction from the Holy Spirit as he witnessed to the young man. They had been talking about how the Americans never came to the aid of the Kurds in Kosovo, where the young man was from, and my uncle told him that he needed to be more informed. But my uncle told him his biggest concern is that our new friend claimed to be an atheist. My uncle told him he could never forgive himself if he did not share the love of Christ with him.

I can't tell you that the young Kurd received Christ that night because he did not, but I know a seed was planted, and we pray that it has been watered through the years. I know Christ called us to be witnesses, not Americans, and we should always look for the opportunity to reach out to all lost and in need.

Life Insight: The Great Commission

Christ told the first disciples,

> *"Follow me, and I will make you fishers of men,"*

Matthew 4:19, NIV

Since then, every Christian has been given that calling. We have to understand that it is our job to,

> *"go out into the highways and hedges and compel them to come in, that my house may be filled."*
>
> Luke 14:23, KJV

While we are in the market, at our jobs, walking down the street, or on a train in Germany, we are to witness Christ.

Jesus came to this earth with a mission: to save the lost. He took his message everywhere he went, and often, he was criticized. Jesus said,

> *"For this cause I came into the world, to bear witness of the truth."*
>
> John 18:37, KJV

Now that Jesus has physically left this earth, we must be his hands and feet. We have to carry on his mission. Too many times, I hear people say, "I'm not a preacher" or "I'm not a missionary." Oh yes, you are! If you call yourself a Christian, it means you are Christ-like. So if you are like Christ, you are a witness, a minister, a teacher, a missionary, a healer, a deliverer, a redeemer. You are everything Christ is because he is in you. No matter who you are—an American, a

Canadian, a European, a carpenter, a schoolteacher, or any other way you categorize yourself—first and foremost, you are a witness.

Oh, people, the harvest is great, and there are truly few workers. We must wake up and understand that God told us to go and make more disciples. It says in the Bible that "The glorious gospel...has been committed to our trust." He has ordained you and me to communicate his good news. He has anointed you to teach the gospel. You never have to fear that you won't have the words to say because it is the anointing you need if you have the Holy Spirit.

> *"You shall receive power after that the Holy Ghost is come upon you; and you shall be witnesses unto me...unto the uttermost part of the earth."*
>
> Acts 1:18, KJV

The power of the Holy Spirit helps us be that witness, so step out of your comfort zone and spread the good news.

Let God's love and compassion fill you so you may see the harvest and go out and be part of God's great commission.

Chapter Thirteen

Grounded

I woke up and looked at the clock. It was 3:15 a.m. I did not have to get up for another hour, but I felt so anxious. I assumed it was because I was leaving for Haiti today. Six others and myself were going on a ten-day mission trip, and I had no idea what was in store. Although this was not my first short-term mission, it was my first to Haiti, a politically unstable country.

I did not bother trying to go back to sleep; instead, I decided I should use this time to pray over the trip. I prayed until I felt some peace from my anxiety. About an hour later, I was ready to go. My mom got up to see me off. As I was getting ready, Mom told me about waking up really early and thinking that the Lord was telling her to pray for all of us and our protection. "Funny," I said. "That happened to me, too."

My dad drove me to the church, where we were to meet the rest of the team. The seven of us piled into two cars with all our gear and drove to the airport in Raleigh. We got checked in and went to the gate. A few of us were hungry and headed to the coffee bar for a light breakfast. We were all excited and ready to get going but had a long wait. Because it was an international flight, we had to be at the airport two hours early. It seemed shorter than it was, and before we knew it, we were loading onto the plane. Vann, Donna, and I were seated on one side, and the rest of the team was across from us. While waiting for the pre-flight check, the three of us began talking. We were all amazed to discover that we all woke up early and needed to pray. Someone commented that we must spiritually have some big things in store for this trip if the Lord was moving all of us to pray this morning. I was starting to get excited now. I could not help but think I was about to be a part of something great.

About ten minutes after we were supposed to leave, the pilot announced they had to fix something on the plane before we could take off. "Just sit back and relax," the pilot said. "We will be on our way as soon as possible." I leaned my head back and fell asleep. I am not much of a morning person, and this morning started too early.

It was almost an hour later, and we were finally on our way. It seemed we had to taxi forever to get to the runway. The pilot told us we were third to take off. From my seat, I could see the first plane take off, then the second plane take off, and we just sat there. Did he not say we were third? I thought to myself.

The pilot returned to the speaker, and we immediately knew something was wrong. He did not sound as professional as earlier. He was fighting to find the words to say. "Um, um, I'm sorry, but we must return to the gate. Everyone will have to go back through security," he sounded shocked and confused.

We all had no idea what to think; everyone was confused. We turned around and headed back to the airport. The pilot came over the speaker again, now sounding shaken, and said, "There has been some kind of terrorist activity, and an American Airlines plane has been flown into the World Trade Center."

Blank—that is what I felt. As I looked around, I realized everyone must be feeling the same way by the look on their faces. The flight attendant near me was in tears. I thought she probably knew someone on that plane because we were on an American Airlines flight.

When we arrived at the gate, everyone gathered their stuff and exited the plane. An airport representative met us, directing us to go to the baggage claim, get our luggage, and leave immediately. "Leave the airport?" we asked. "Yes," they answered. "There will be no flights until further notice."

Our problem was that we did not have a car at the airport. We had been dropped off more than four hours ago and were two hours from home. So Brandon checked into renting a car, but they were all out. We started making calls to find a ride home. I just wanted to talk to my mom; I was scared and confused. The worst thing was that we still did not know what was happening because all the airport TVs and radios were shut off.

Finally, we had someone on the way, so we waited for what seemed like forever. News crews were all over the place interviewing people. Someone from the Associated Press asked to interview me, and I consented if he told us what was happening. He proceeded to say to us, and I could not believe it.

On our way back home, we listened to the radio to hear the events. As much as I wanted to feel something, I was still blank. Finally, I arrived home, fell into my mother's arms, and started to cry. I guess I was in shock.

Like everyone in the U.S., I was glued to the TV for the next week; to this day, it is hard to believe something like this could happen to us.

I cannot help but think that the Lord was looking out for our team. The Lord knew we were about to face something devastating and wanted to prepare our hearts. I believe he woke us up that morning and told us to pray. If we had not prayed, our flight would have taken off at the right time, and we could have been stranded somewhere between Raleigh and Haiti, trying to find a way home. Instead, I was at home with my family, comforted with my Lord's peace.

Life Insight: Protected

My pastor never lets us go on a mission trip without learning Psalm 91 because it is a promise of God for our protection. Although mission trips are not the only time I use that Psalm, I never leave the house without it on my heart. The psalmist praised God for this promise, telling us that if we chose as he did to live under God's wings, God would be our refuge and our fortress and would also deliver us from our enemies. God tells us not to be afraid of anything. Psalm 91:7 says,

> *"A thousand shall fall at thy side, and ten thousand at they right hand; but it shall not come nigh thee."*
>
> KJV

So, no matter what is happening around you or who is falling into the enemy's hands, we do not need to worry. Verse 8 tells us,

> *"Only with thine eyes shalt thou behold and see the reward of the wicked."*
>
> KJV

Do you understand what this is telling us? He is saying that we would only see the destruction of the wicked, but it would bring us no harm. Understand, people, we live in a world that Satan and his dominion rule. Adam saw that when he gave in to Satan in the Garden of Eden. I hear so many people say, "Why does God allow evil things to happen?" God does not allow these things to happen—man does. Man was the one who gave the keys of this world to Satan and made him the prince of our world.

Let's look at Psalm 91:9,

> "Because thou hast made the Lord, which is my refuge, even the Most High, thy habitation."
>
> KJV

All these promises found in the ninety-first psalm are ours when we make God our habitation, the place we live and move and have our being. Verse 15 says,

> "He shall call upon me, and I will answer him; I will be with him in trouble; I will deliver him and honour him."
>
> KJV

Verse 16 says he will give us a long life. Through our covenant with Jesus and what he did on the cross, we now have dominion over the things on this earth, and we are not to fear our enemies—even ones we never suspect.

Chapter Fourteen

Here We Go Again

It's February 2002, and we are trying it again; we're heading to Haiti and hoping we make it this time. The last time we tried this trip was September 11, 2001. On this trip, there were only four of us: Brandon, Donna, Darlene, and me. We boarded the plane, and this is as far as we got last time. Brandon, Donna, and Darlene were in the row in front of me, and I was in the last row on the plane. A gentleman sat down in the row across from me and buckled his seat belt. The flight attendants ran up and down the aisles, looking for overhead bins not yet full to stuff in one last bag. One of the male flight attendants stopped at my row and asked the man across from me if he would mind moving. The gentleman was Haitian and only knew a little English. The flight attendant then went and got a female attendant who spoke Haitian Creole. She then asked the man if he would mind moving. He refused to move. They spent twenty minutes or so trying to convince him to move, but he refused each time. "I paid for seat. I not move," he would say in his broken English. Finally, the first flight attendant said to forget it because we were already thirty minutes behind schedule. The whole time, I was thinking maybe I should move because, for some reason, they did not want this guy to sit there, and I was sitting across from him.

Now we were on our way to the runway, getting ready to take off, and you will never believe what happened next: he moved! He moved up a row to the seat across from Darlene, and we were getting ready to take off! I could see the flight attendant who asked him to move seated in his jump seat. I waved at him to get his attention and hurriedly said, "He moved, he moved." The attendant immediately jumped up and got on the phone to talk to the pilot. "He moved, and either you get him off this plane, or you get me off," he told the pilot. I'm going with you, I thought. Then, the pilot came over the overhead speaker and announced, "We are having a little mechanical difficulty, and we will have to go back to the gate. We will be on our way as soon as we get the problem fixed."

On our way back, Darlene and Donna looked back at me, and I exaggerated by looking at him so that they would know to watch him. Then he kicked his shoe off and pulled something out of his shoe. Of course, the first thing that comes to my mind is, "Didn't the terrorists from 9/11 pull the weapons out of their shoes?" He then put whatever he had taken out of his shoe behind his belt buckle. The flight attendant then kneeled beside me and started reaching behind my seat. I looked back to see what he was doing, and he pulled out a fire extinguisher and stayed ready to hit the guy with it. Donna told Darlene to put on her sunglasses just in case the flight attendant sprayed the guy; Donna grabbed her backpack from under her seat and was ready to swing it at him; and Brandon (ex-special forces Vietnam Vet) just crossed his arms sat back, and watched the scene. I grabbed the pillow beside me and buried my face, and at that point, I was unsure if I was laughing or crying; I knew I wanted off that plane. The flight attendant started patting my arm, trying to let me know everything would be okay. Then, the attendant moved me to the jump seat, so I had to lean past the wall to see what was happening.

As soon as we arrived at the gate, the door flew open, and three security guards came flying down the aisle, grabbed the guy, flung him across the seat in front of Donna and Darlene, handcuffed him, and dragged him off the plane. Then, a gentleman from the FAA interviewed Donna, the flight attendant, and me. After all that, we headed back to the runway like nothing happened. I had to ask the flight attendant why he wanted to move the guy in the first place. The flight attendant said he watched the guy get pulled during a security search and give the security officers a hard time. This is why he did not want him near the back door right behind him.

The next day, we were at the domestic airport, waiting to catch a single-engine plane to Pignon, when a gentleman approached me.

"Were you not on the flight from Miami yesterday?"

"Yeah, I was," I answered.

"What in the world was going on?" he asked. After telling him the story, he said to hang on because he had to get his buddies to hear this.

After repeating the story to my new audience, one wanted to take a picture of Donna, Darlene, and me. The Charlie's Angels, he called us and said, "Our heroes!" By the way, the guy was not a terrorist; he was trying to smuggle drugs.

Life Insight: Nothing to Fear

What's the old saying? We have nothing to fear but fear itself. I know on that day, on that plane, I was scared to death. The only thing that was on my mind was 9/11. This was the exact flight and trip we were supposed to take that day, and fear jumped over me. I soon realized I had not let the peace of God and his Word settle in my heart.

God's Word has so much to say on the subject of fear. Psalm 27:1-3 says,

> *"The Lord is my light and my salvation; whom shall I fear? The Lord is the strength of my life; of whom shall I be afraid? When the wicked, even mine enemies and my foes, came upon me to eat up my flesh, they stumbled and fell. Though an host should encamp against me, my heart shall not fear: though war should rise against me, in this will I be confident."*
>
> KJV

Psalm 56:9 says,

> "When I cry unto thee, then shall mine enemies turn back; this I know: for God is for me."
>
> KJV

And Psalm 46:1 says,

> "God is our refuge and strength, a very present help in trouble."
>
> KJV

These are only a few Scriptures assuring us that no matter what comes against us, God will be on our side.

I love the story in 2 Kings 6. It is the story of the prophet Elisha and how the King of Syria was pretty ticked at him because he was able to help Israel through God's prophecy. The King of Syria went after him, and Elisha and his servant awoke early one morning, and their enemy surrounded them.

Verse 15 says,

> "And when the servant of the man of God was risen early, and gone forth, behold, an host compassed the city both

> *with horses and chariots. And his servant said unto him, 'Alas, my master! How shall we do?'"*
>
> KJV

Elisha's servant was terrified and asked Elisha, "What in the world are we, the two of us, going to do about this?" Elisha's reply is found in verses 16-17,

> *"And he answered, 'Fear not: for they that be with us are more than they that be with them.' And Elisha prayed, and said, 'Lord, I pray thee, open his eyes, that he may see.' And the Lord opened the eyes of the young man; and he saw: and, behold, the mountain was full of horses and chariots of fire round about Elisha."*
>
> KJV

Here was a situation that seemed impossible to overcome. They were surrounded in the physical; death was imminent, but, and I do mean but, God was on their side. Elisha wanted his servant to know that God was more powerful than anything, so he asked God to open his eyes to what the supernatural beheld: victory and dominion over the enemy. This is also what God is trying to tell us today. We have victory in him, and knowing we have victory and dominion means we have no reason to fear.

"For God hath not given us the spirit of fear; but of power, and of love, and of a sound mind"
2 Timothy 1:7, KJV

Will I fear again? Maybe, but I pray that my faith will overcome my fear and that the power of God and his love will help me overcome it. Because greater is he that is in me than he that is in the world. (1 John 4:4, paraphrased).

Chapter Fifteen

My Miracle on the Mountain

So, my family—parents, sister, brother-in-law, nephew, Melanie, and I—packed up for a five-day adventure at Hungry Mother State Park in Virginia. Yes, that's the real name. My parents brought their camper, which comfortably slept four. They planned to house themselves and my four-year-old nephew. My sister and brother-in-law went out with a four-man tent, complete with cots and all the bells and whistles. Melanie and I? We decided to "rough it" with one-man tents, sleeping on the ground. Okay, okay, we were just a few feet away from my parents' air-conditioned camper, and we did have pads under our sleeping bags, but still, we were practically wild campers for five days!

The park was stunning, with a lovely stream winding through the campsites and a perfect lake for canoeing, paddle boating, and swimming. There was even a restaurant on the lake when we got tired of our hotdog and hamburger diet. But, of course, it rained almost the entire time. Did we let that stop us? Absolutely not! We made a quick trip to the nearest Wal-Mart (there's always one nearby), and we had a tent shelter over our picnic table and grill. We were officially out of the rain for meals. We swam in the misty rain, rode paddleboats, and even had a fishing adventure where my nephew caught his first "fish"—which, let's be honest, was more of a minnow.

On the third day, the rain finally decided to give us a break, and we were eager to explore the hiking trails. So, with a map, some water, and hours before sunset, Mom, Shelly, Coy, Melanie, and I set off to stretch our legs. After a short but "long" walk for Coy, Mom, Shelly, and Coy returned to camp, leaving Melanie and me to tackle Hungry Mother Mountain on our own.

We hiked for hours, marveling at the beautiful trees, flowers, and winding trails. At one point, we reached a narrow part of the trail that snaked around a ravine, with a steep drop on one side and a mountainside on the other. Suddenly, my right foot slipped! Melanie reached back, but she barely grabbed my arm. Then, out of nowhere, something yanked me up by my right arm and set me back on my feet. Melanie turned to me, wide-eyed. "I didn't catch you," she said, more as a question than a statement. "No, something grabbed my right arm," I replied, feeling sore. "Do you think it was your guardian angel?" she asked. "It's the only way I can explain it," I said. We were both stunned. I'm convinced that's precisely what happened, and whenever I doubt, I remember that near-slip and feel reassured.

But our adventure wasn't over yet—we got lost. At first, we weren't too worried because we had a map (which turned out to be pretty useless), and we hadn't strayed from the groomed trail. How lost could we be, right? Hours later, with the sun beginning to set and no water left, we started to get nervous. "What do we do if it gets dark?" Melanie asked, trying not to sound worried. "Well, since we don't have a flashlight and we're deep in the woods, I guess we'd have to sit tight until morning," I said, secretly praying it wouldn't come to that.

Meanwhile, back at camp, my parents were getting distraught. They had chatted with a couple camping nearby who had mentioned getting lost on the trails just the day before. My mom decided that if we weren't back by sunset, she'd go straight to the ranger's house, but for now, she was praying we'd turn up soon.

Finally, Melanie and I recognized the first trail we'd been on and knew we were almost home. I decided to run ahead and let everyone know we were okay, leaving Melanie to limp back to camp with her blistered feet. When I reached camp, it was dark, and my mom was nearly in tears until she saw me. We were exhausted and didn't want anything but sleep. We slept like rocks that night and were incredibly grateful it was in our sleeping bags and not on the mountain trail!

Life Insight: Stand Firm

As Christians, one of the most important things we must learn is how to stand firm in our faith—how to dig in our heels and stay rooted, no matter what life throws at us. When Melanie and I found ourselves lost on that mountain, it would have been easy to let fear take over, especially as the sun started dipping lower in the sky. But deep down, we knew we'd eventually find our way back. Sure, there were moments when it felt like nightfall might beat us to it, but we held on to the belief that God's Word is accurate and that He'd keep His promise to protect us.

Isn't it interesting how we sometimes only remember to lean on our faith when in a tight spot? We have this incredible power at our disposal, but we only dust it off when we're desperate. Paul gives us a solid reminder in 1 Corinthians 16:13:

> *"Be on your guard; stand firm in the faith; be courageous; be strong."*
>
> NIV

He's basically saying, "Hey, pay attention! Life is moving fast, and a lot is happening around you. If you're not careful, you can lose yourself—and your faith—in the hustle and bustle."

God does not want us to go through the motions. He wants us to be vigilant, to watch over our faith like it's the most precious thing we have—because it is! He knows how easily we can get swept up in the latest trends or ideas, just like Paul mentions in Ephesians 4:14 (KJV) when he talks about being *"carried about by every wind of doctrine."* It's easy to get distracted, to let the world's noise drown out God's still, small voice. But that's precisely why He calls us to be people of courage and faith. He wants us to hold on tight to our commitment and remember why we chose to follow Him in the first place.

And why did we choose to follow Him? Because we're after something real—something the world can't offer. We're after that true, everlasting, unconditional love that only God can provide. We're looking for the peace that passes all understanding, the kind of happiness that isn't based on circumstances, and a deep and abiding joy. Let's be honest—nothing on this earth can bring that kind of joy. Sure, plenty of things can make us happy for a moment, but they're fleeting. The joy that comes from God? That's the real deal, and it's eternal.

Paul doesn't stop there, though. He also tells us to be strong—but here's the thing: the word "strong" in this context means "to be strengthened." God isn't just telling us to toughen up and figure it out alone. He's offering to be our strength, lift, and support us when we feel weak. He wants to encourage and remind us that we don't have to go through this life relying solely on our power. We can let Him strengthen us; when we do, we can stand firm, even in the face of the toughest challenges.

Let's be real—being a Christian isn't always easy. There are days when it feels like it would be so much simpler to throw in the towel and go with the flow of the world. The world can be pretty persuasive, after all. But where would that lead us? Down a path of destruction, pain, and defeat. And that's not what God wants for His children. He wants so much more for us—He wants us to be blessed, healed, delivered, and set free. He wants us to experience the fullness of life that He has to offer. Our Father loves us deeply, and He wants nothing but the absolute best for us.

So, when life gets tough and the road ahead seems uncertain, remember what Paul says in Ephesians 6:10:

> *"Be strong in the Lord and in his mighty power."*
>
> NIV

Trust that God is with you, that He's guiding you through the challenges, and that He's going to lead you safely home. No matter what comes your way, you can stand firm in your faith, knowing that God's got you in His hands.

Chapter Sixteen

A Coastal Escapade: When Birds Attack (Sort of)

It all started with one of those phone calls from Melanie that simply said, "Want to do something fun today?" You know the kind — deceptively casual, yet almost guaranteed to end in some memorable mischief. Within the hour, we were tossing beach bags into the backseat and heading east to the North Carolina coast, because why not? Wilmington was calling, and we were answering.

Our first stop was the charming streets of downtown Wilmington. We hopped on a horse-drawn trolley tour, clip-clopping past historic homes with wraparound porches that practically begged us to sit a spell. The guide's stories were almost as rich as the scent of jasmine drifting through the warm air.

Next, we found a cute little bistro where we devoured plates of shrimp and grits that deserved their own standing ovation. Then we strolled along the waterfront, letting the breeze tangle our hair and laughing about nothing and everything.

Eventually, we decided to make our way toward the ferry for a little water adventure. Before boarding, we drove to the terminal parking lot and waited, windows down, sun streaming in, dreaming of sandy toes and saltwater. That's when the real show began.

See, Melanie had a bright idea. Too bright, in hindsight. "Hey!" she chirped. "I've got some leftover bread. I'm going to feed the seagulls!"

Now, a normal person might say, "Maybe not, Mel. This is how Hitchcock movies start." But I froze — not from courtesy, but from sheer personal terror. You see, ever since I was a kid and my aunt thought it would be fine to watch *The Birds* while I pretended to be asleep on the couch (spoiler: I was *wide awake* and traumatized), birds and I have had an unspoken agreement. They stay over there; I stay over here.

But Melanie was already out of the car, bread in hand, standing smack in the middle of the lot like Snow White summoning woodland creatures. Only, these weren't dainty bluebirds. These were seagulls. Big, loud, greedy seagulls.

It took about 2.5 seconds for the first gull to swoop down. Then another. And another. Suddenly there were hundreds. Melanie shrieked — not a delicate squeal, but a full-on horror movie scream that echoed across the asphalt.

And what did I do? The loyal, steadfast friend that I am? I burst into laughter so hard I nearly fell out of the car. Because that's true friendship — laughing first, helping second. (Okay, helping maybe third in this case because my bird phobia had me plastered to the opposite car door like it was made of Velcro.)

Finally, between my gasping giggles, I managed to yell, "RUN FOR THE CAR!"

Melanie bolted, arms flailing, bread forgotten, birds chasing her like she was the final contestant on a bizarre game show. She threw herself inside the car, slammed the door, and we both sat there — breathless, wide-eyed, then dissolved into hysterics.

We waited it out, our nerves as fried as the hush puppies we'd had at lunch, until the ferry finally arrived and we could escape our feathered foes. By the time we were skimming across the water, sun setting in a blaze of pink and gold, it was all we could do to replay the scene and howl with laughter all over again.

In the end, we did walk along the beach, toes sinking into cool sand, hearts full. Because that's the best part of days like these — not just the pretty sights or good food, but the way one wild, slightly terrifying memory turns into the story we'll tell for years.

And yes, next time, I'm packing a sign: **"Please do not feed the birds. For my sake."**

Life Insight: Bird Drama & Bigger Lessons, Letting Perfect Love Chase Out Fear

Isn't it something how fear can shrink our world?

That day on the coast, fear looked like a squawking mob of seagulls — but the truth is, fear takes all sorts of shapes. Sometimes it looks like stepping into an unfamiliar season, or loving again after you have been hurt. Sometimes it is daring to dream, risking disappointment, or letting people see the real you.

Fear tells us to stay in the car. To play it safe. To watch through the window while life dances (or in this case, flaps) by.

But as I sat there, doubled over in laughter yet still rooted to my seat by an old terror, I was reminded how often fear holds us back from fully living. It isolates us, magnifies the worst possibilities, and convinces us that staying put is safer than stepping out.

Yet even then — even in the hiding — God is with us. His love does not shame us for our fears; it wraps us up in understanding. It coaxes us gently forward.

1 John 4:18 says:

> "There is no fear in love; but perfect love casts out fear, because fear involves torment. But he who fears has not been made perfect in love."
>
> NKJV

God's perfect love does not just tolerate our fear. It *casts it out*. His love floods the dark corners where fear has made a nest and sends it packing.

That day by the ferry, I did not conquer my bird phobia. (Let us be real — if anything, it got a little more dramatic!) But you know what? I also did not let it steal my joy. Melanie and I still laughed ourselves silly, still rode that ferry, still soaked in the sunset and salty breeze.

And maybe that is how courage grows — not by waiting for fear to disappear, but by refusing to let it stop you from living the moments God has written for you.

So friend, what does your "parking lot full of birds" look like? What fear is trying to keep you stuck?

Today, let God's perfect love flood that place. Let it loosen your grip on control, calm your racing heart, and whisper that you are safe in Him. Because with Jesus, you can take the next step — trembling maybe, but never alone.

Chapter Seventeen
Midnight Snack

It was our last night in Haiti, and I was lying in bed, soaking wet with sweat. We had to spend our last night in Port-au-Prince, which I always dread. The capital of Haiti is always at least twenty degrees hotter than the mountains. Donna, Darlene, and I were sharing a room, and somehow they managed to fall asleep. As for myself, I was lying there dreaming of home. It was wintertime there, and I was thinking of heading straight for the shower as soon as I entered my door. Ah, there is nothing like home: air-conditioning, indoor plumbing, and exterminators—now that's the life.

While I was daydreaming—or is it nightdreaming?—I started to hear a noise. I went searching for my flashlight, and I remembered Darlene had borrowed it.

"Darlene," trying to wake her, "Darlene, do you have food in your suitcase?" I asked.

"Yeah, some crackers," she answered groggily.

"Listen," I told her. We got quiet again and listened to the crinkle of plastic.

"Ah shoot, I was going to eat those," she answered.

Darlene got out of bed with the flashlight and headed over to her suitcase. There was her culprit, eating to his heart's content. She picked up the box of snack crackers, mouse and all, from her open suitcase and took him to the other side of the room. After running into starving dogs, chickens, and children this trip, we just sat there listening to him eat. None of us had the heart to take the food away from him. At least something in Haiti was eating good tonight.

Life Insight: Blessed or Cursed

Deuteronomy 30:19 tells us we have a choice to be blessed or cursed. So, what is God telling us here? He is telling us that if we choose him, then we will be blessed. We will be blessed if we decide to follow the Word of God. We will be so blessed that everything we set our hands to will prosper (Psalm 1:3). Take a few minutes and read Deuteronomy 28 and see what all God promises us when we follow after him and his Word. He also tells us in Deuteronomy 30:20 that he is the length of our days if we choose to cleave to him. We make choices every day. We choose what to wear, eat, and many other things. It is just as important to decide to take up our cross daily and choose to follow him. He will reward that choice and bless us for it. On the other hand, if you do not choose God and obey his Word, then you also have the option to be cursed. While reading Deuteronomy 28, you had to have noticed all the curses that followed, and many people believe this is cruel.

It is not cruel; God does not want any of his children to suffer pain or the consequences of wrong choices. It happens daily because we choose the wrong road and do not turn around until it is too late.

Our wonderful forefathers chose to follow after God. Our country was built on the foundations of the Word of God, and our laws are based on the Word—the Ten Commandments. Because of this choice, we are blessed people. If you do not see that, you must visit some of these other countries, such as Haiti, one of the poorest countries in our world. Haiti is an excellent example of a country that does not choose God. The country is saturated with voodoo and an ungodly government. The government has no desire to help its people, and it does not have the foundation of the Word that has sustained the United States and made it so blessed.

We must be like Joshua and proclaim, "As for me and my house, we will serve the Lord." If you choose to believe God's Word, he promises:

> *"I call heaven and earth to record this day against you, that I have set before you life and death, blessing and cursing: therefore choose life, that both thou and thy seed may live: That thou mayest love the Lord thy God, and that thou mayest obey his voice, and that thou mayest cleave*

> *unto him: for he is thy life, and the length of thy days: that thou mayest dwell in the land which the Lord sware unto thy fathers, to Abraham, to Issac, and to Jacob, to give them."*
>
> Deuteronomy 30:19-20, KJV

Make your choice today. Choose wisely and be blessed.

Chapter Eighteen

God, I Know You Can Move Mountains, But Can You Help Me Get Down One?

Eight of us decided to go four-wheeling in West Virginia one weekend. We left on a Friday evening, driving two SUVs, each pulling a trailer loaded with four-wheelers. It was long after dark when we arrived at the campground, but that didn't stop us from setting up camp. Most of us hit the sack quickly, but a few brave souls decided to take a night ride.

The following day, we jumped on the bikes and headed to a local restaurant for breakfast. What's so cool about this town is that it is completely set up for riders. All the campgrounds and restaurants are right off the trails, and no one cares how dirty you are when you show up to eat. After breakfast, we returned to the campsite to regroup and hit our first trail.

We weren't even a few yards down the path when Vann's bike started acting up. He fiddled with the plugs but decided not to risk breaking down, so we turned back. Vann left his bike at camp, and the two younger girls doubled up on one four-wheeler. We rode for about an hour more before the four-wheeler I was on decided it had enough. It started losing power and then just cut off completely.

Everyone had zoomed ahead and left me behind, but when they realized I was missing, they doubled back to find me and Gary trying to figure out what was wrong. We tied my bike to Vann's four-wheeler with nothing else to do, and he towed me back. Now, the only problem with Vann pulling me was the mountains. Yes, mountains. Vann was pulling my bike by a rope, and I had to trust him not to send me flying off a cliff. We went up mountains, down mountains, and even over railroad trestles that were at least twenty-five feet above the ground.

I was yelling at Vann to slow down the whole time, but that didn't do much good. Finally, I started squeezing my brakes and yanking him back, determined to slow him down one way or another. I was praying the entire time, thinking, *I am getting way too old for this kind of stuff.* Is it not funny how the older you get, the less nerve you have? Or maybe you just get smarter with age. Anyway, I promised the Lord that as soon as I made it back to camp, I would never get back on a bike again.

So, we made it back to camp in one piece, and of course, we decided it was time for lunch. And guess what I did? Yep, you guessed it—I got right back on a four-wheeler. We were headed to another restaurant this time, and Vann decided to take a shortcut. As it turned out, the shortcut was straight up a mountainside called the Stair Steps. "But don't worry," Vann said, "We only have to go halfway up and then hop back on a trail."

Well, I was the last to go up, and wouldn't you know it, my bike hit a rut, and I almost flipped it. There I was, hanging on for dear life, trying to keep the bike from rolling down the mountain with me in tow. As I waited for help, all I could think was, *You are an idiot.*

I did eventually make it back to camp, and I haven't been four-wheeling since. Now, I've traded in that adrenaline rush for something a bit safer—competition pistol shooting!

Life Insight: Me Again, Lord

Do you ever feel like a complete goof because you keep making the same silly mistakes, like riding a four-wheeler up treacherous mountainsides? Or maybe, like me, you find yourself repeatedly asking God for help or forgiveness after stumbling over the same issues time and time again. It can be frustrating to realize you are making the same blunders, but here's the thing: even when we mess up, God's mercies are new every single day (Lamentations 3:22-23). Isn't that amazing?

Take Paul, for example. In Romans 7, he's pretty candid about his struggles. He's trying to live right, but he keeps finding himself doing the very things he preaches against. He says,

> "O wretched man that I am! Who will rescue me from this body of death?"
>
> Romans 7:24, NIV

I get where Paul is coming from—sometimes, I find myself stuck in the same patterns despite knowing better.

But here is the good news: we are not stuck with our mistakes. God is not up there with a big, judgmental finger wagging at us. Instead, He offers us a hand to lift us and a heart full of grace. I am not saying this means we should take sin lightly or use grace as a free pass to keep making the same errors. I am saying that we have a Savior who forgives, is patient with us, and helps us overcome our shortcomings. Our Savior helps us move mountains—and yes, even helps us down from those precarious ones we've climbed up!

So, the next time you feel like you're on a never-ending loop of mistakes, remember that God's grace is always ready to meet you where you are, and His help is there to guide you through. Keep pressing on, knowing that every stumble is just another opportunity to experience His boundless love and forgiveness.

If you can't laugh at your own wrong turn, at least take a picture!

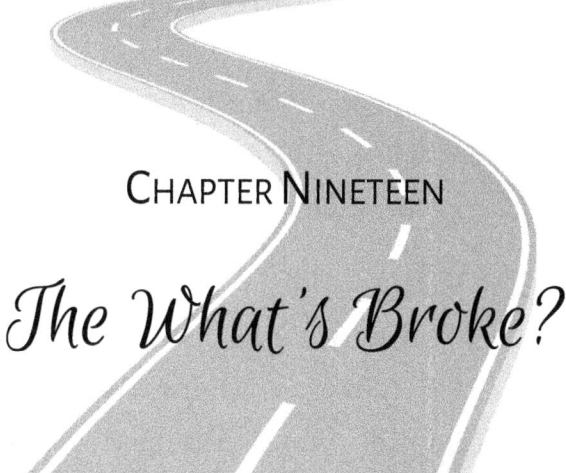

Chapter Nineteen

The What's Broke?

Gary and I were on our honeymoon, setting sail from Port Canaveral for a five-day cruise to Mexico. After the whirlwind of wedding craziness, we couldn't wait to just relax and enjoy ourselves. It was our first cruise, so we had no idea what to expect. We got to our cabin, and, well, let's just say it was a bit cozier than we'd imagined. I remember hearing a comedian on the ship joke, "You didn't realize that the picture in the brochure was actual size, did you?" Spot on! At least we had a huge window, which I was really grateful for—except for the day I got seasick. That day, the window and I weren't on the best of terms!

We were excited to watch the ship pull into port at Key West on the second day. We got up early, headed to the top deck, and...no Key West. We were supposed to dock at 7 a.m., but it was 6:50, and all we saw was endless ocean. Finally, the captain announced that we were only cruising with one propeller—yep, the other one had taken a break. So, we were chugging along at half speed. He cheerfully informed us we'd arrive in Key West around 9 a.m., and there'd be a dive team waiting to check things out.

We finally left Key West at midnight instead of the planned 2 p.m. departure. By then, we'd learned that because of the propeller problem, we wouldn't make it to Cozumel. Instead, we were headed to the Bahamas. The crew had managed to fix the propeller temporarily, but the permanent fix would have to wait until we got to the ship's home dock in the Bahamas.

Of course, we were a little bummed, but Gary just laughed and said, "With you around, what else could I expect?" He's convinced I'm some mishap magnet, but I'm not so sure. I mean, just because he had to propose to me in a hospital room instead of that fancy restaurant doesn't necessarily mean it's my fault... right?

So, no Mexico for us, but we did make it to the Bahamas. We didn't get to ride dune buggies through the jungles of Costa Maya, but we did go snorkeling off the beautiful island of Coco Cay. And honestly, the best part? I got to spend the first week of the rest of my life with the man of my dreams. Oh, and let's not forget the all-you-can-eat buffet—no matter the destination, that's a win!

Life Insight: Other Plans?

How many times have you made plans only to have them completely derailed? It's happened to me more times than I can count, and not just with simple things like vacations. We all have this idea of where our life is headed, what we want to do, or who we want to be when we grow up. But I don't know about you—God seemed to have a totally different path in mind for me. Proverbs 16:9 (NIV) says, "In their hearts humans plan their course, but the Lord establishes their steps."

Take Jonah, for example—a classic case of someone trying to go their own way. In Jonah 1:1, God tells him to go to Nineveh and preach against the city, but Jonah has other plans and hops on a boat to Tarshish instead. Spoiler alert: it doesn't go well for him. As Proverbs 19:21 reminds us,

> "Many are the plans in a person's heart, but it is the Lord's purpose that prevails."
>
> NIV

After Jonah gets thrown overboard and spends three days in the belly of a giant fish, he starts to see things God's way. He finally heads to Nineveh and, by declaring God's word, saves the city from destruction. He learned the hard way about the importance of obedience (Jonah 1-3).

Hopefully, most of us won't need such a dramatic lesson to realize that God knows best. The Bible reassures us in Jeremiah 29:11-13:

> "'For I know the plans I have for you,' declares the Lord, 'plans to prosper you and not to harm you, plans to give

you hope and a future. Then you will call on me, come and pray to me, and I will listen. You will seek me and find me when you seek me with all your heart.'"

NIV

Trusting God with our plans is the best thing we can do. Proverbs 16:3 (NIV) tells us that if we commit our plans to the Lord, they will succeed. Psalm 37:4 reminds us that God will give us the desires of our hearts, but only if we truly believe.

Gary and I put our trust in God when we found ourselves in the middle of the ocean with a broken propeller. Sure, we didn't make it to Mexico, but at least we didn't spend our honeymoon in the belly of a whale!

Chapter Twenty
The Honeymoon Reef

Gary and I were on our honeymoon. If you remember back with me, we didn't make it to Mexico like we planned. Yep—our ship rerouted to the Bahamas instead. Life lesson: even on your honeymoon, detours happen. We had dreamed of Mexico, but our cruise ship ended up detouring to the Bahamas instead.

It wasn't part of the plan, but I was excited anyway. The beach, the sun, the blue-green water all felt like paradise.

One of the excursions offered was snorkeling. I love to swim, so I signed up without a second thought. In my mind, it was the perfect adventure for newlyweds. Swim together, see colorful fish, make a memory. Simple.

What I didn't know was that my new husband had been carrying fear with him for years. A fear he had never told me about.

We strapped on our life jackets and headed out into the cove. The reef was farther out, and we started swimming toward it. I was eager to see what was waiting beneath the surface. For me, swimming was freedom. For Gary, I would soon learn, it was something entirely different.

At first, he stayed close. But as I swam a little ahead, I realized he wasn't beside me anymore. I turned around, and that's when I saw him.

The look on his face stopped me cold. He was pale, stiff, and terrified. The kind of fear that you don't mistake for anything else.

I swam back as fast as I could and grabbed onto his lifejacket. My mind went through every possible danger. "Are you hurt? Did something sting you? Did a shark pass by?"

He shook his head, still trying to find words. Finally, with a voice tight and trembling, he said, "I hate the water."

That confession hit me harder than the waves lapping around us. My strong, confident, new husband, the man who could handle almost anything, was undone by the sea.

That's when he told me the story. As a boy, he had nearly drowned. The fear of water had followed him into adulthood. He could swim if he had to, but it wasn't strength. It was survival. Every moment in the water feltlike a fight.

There we were, far from shore, me wide-eyed in surprise, him frozen in fear. I looked him in the eyes and asked, "Do you trust me?"

"Yes," he said.

"Then trust the life jacket. It's got you."

So, we stayed right where we were. Bobbing up and down with the tide. Letting the water hold us instead of fight us.

Slowly, I could see the panic in his eyes soften. His grip on me loosened. His breathing steadied. Minute by minute, his confidence grew—not in himself, but in the thing designed to keep him afloat.

Eventually, he was ready to move again. Together, we swam to the reef. We didn't stay long, but we stayed long enough. Long enough for him to see the fish. Long enough for me to know he had conquered something deep inside.

Back on shore, I told him how proud I was. He had faced his fears for me because he knew how much snorkeling meant to me. Later, I went back out alone and soaked in the beauty of the reef. But the real memory wasn't what I saw in the water, it was what I saw in him.

Love doesn't always look like flowers, candlelight, or perfect moments. Sometimes it looks like a husband staring down a fear so his wife can smile. Sometimes it looks like floating in the water until courage comes back.

Love shows up in ways you don't expect. And if you're paying attention, you'll see it.

Life Insight: Learning to Float in Faith

Fear is powerful. It convinces us that we'll sink even when we're being held up. It whispers worst-case scenarios until we freeze.

Gary's fear was water. Yours may be something else: failure, rejection, change, the unknown. We all have a "reef" that feels too far to reach.

What Gary needed that day was not more strength. He needed trust. He needed to believe that the life jacket could do what it was designed to do.

That's what God invites us to do every single day.

Isaiah 41:10 reminds us,

> *"Don't be afraid, for I am with you. Don't be discouraged, for I am your God. I will strengthen you and help you. I will hold you up with my victorious right hand."*
>
> NLT

God doesn't ask you to muscle through your fears alone. He asks you to trust Him. To lean into His strength. To believe He will keep you afloat even when the water feels overwhelming.

What fear are you carrying today? What "reef" have you avoided because you weren't sure you could make it?

God is your life jacket. You may still feel the waves. You may still see the deep waters around you. But you won't sink when you trust the One who holds you up.

Chapter Twenty-One

Horsing Around

Oh, there's nothing quite like the "luxury" of modern transportation in Haiti. We were at the mission in Rang, waiting for our ride to Cerca Carvajal. The plan was to head over to a church there for some ministry work. Cerca Carvajal is only about five miles away, but that feels like a marathon in Haiti. The roads are an adventure in themselves—straight up and down mountains, with rain-carved crevices and boulders big enough to give you a whole new perspective on "off-roading." And if it's the rainy season? Well, forget it—those roads turn into mud pits that could swallow you whole.

Finally, after waiting an hour, our rides arrived. But in Haiti, an hour late is right on time. The Haitians aren't exactly in a hurry—ever. Our rides were the most pitiful little horses I'd ever seen. I couldn't help but protest, convinced these poor creatures wouldn't even be able to carry us. "Oh, yes, they're strong mountain horses, no problem," they assured us, somehow talking me into it. Donna took one look and flat-out refused to ride, deciding she'd rather walk. The rest of us climbed aboard these horses with "saddles" made of feed sacks stuffed with hay and tied on with rope. Let's just say I wasn't feeling particularly secure.

We set off at a snail's pace, with the breathtaking Haitian countryside as our backdrop—if you could manage to enjoy it while bouncing along. We finally made it to the church, where we had a wonderful service that lasted for hours. I couldn't help but chuckle, thinking that back home, people would've been tapping their watches a couple of hours ago, hinting that it was time to wrap things up before the restaurants got too crowded.

After the service, the church ladies treated us to a delicious meal, and the children sang for us. But by the time we were ready to head back, it was pitch black outside. With no electricity in the area, you couldn't see your hand in front of your face. They had to grab chairs from the church to help us mount the horses again since our makeshift saddles didn't have stirrups. Poor Donna, who had walked on the way there, decided that riding back was her only option. A few of our Haitian friends walked alongside us, carrying a flashlight to light the way.

We were more than halfway home, navigating a steep hill, when suddenly, I felt my "saddle" slip. I knew I needed to jump off, but swinging my leg over with no stirrups and being in a skirt wasn't exactly easy. Before I could do anything, I was tumbling off the horse. I tried to twist so I'd land on my bottom, but instead, I hit the ground on my side, with a rock digging right into my lower back. There was a lot of shouting and running as everyone realized I'd fallen. I was lying there, trying to assess if I could still move everything when suddenly, two or three Haitians yanked me up. I wanted to tell them to slow down and make sure I wasn't seriously hurt, but they didn't understand.

Brandon was yelling, "Help me off this horse," so he could check on me. Everyone was in a panic because if someone had gotten seriously hurt, we were nowhere near a doctor or hospital. Finally, amidst all the chaos, I convinced everyone that I was okay and that I'd be just fine walking the rest of the way home. I couldn't help but feel a bit embarrassed, though. It wasn't the first time I'd fallen off a horse, but at least in the past, I could say I was thrown—not just that I fell. It didn't help when I got home, and my dad said, "I'm so ashamed that my daughter, a native Texan, fell off a horse." I'll never live it down!

Life Insight: I've Fallen and I Can't Get Up

How many of us have made a mistake or two since giving our lives to the Lord? Of course, none of us has sinned since then, right? We both know that's not true. First John 1:8-2:2 (NIV) tells us:

> "Suppose we claim we are without sin. Then we are fooling ourselves. The truth is not in us. But God is faithful and fair. If we admit that we have sinned, He will forgive us our sins. He will forgive every wrong thing we have

done. He will make us pure. If we say we have not sinned, we are calling God a liar. His word has no place in our lives. My dear children, I'm writing this to you so that you will not sin. But suppose someone does sin. Then we have one who speaks to the Father in our defense. He stands up for us. He is Jesus Christ, the Blameless One. He gave His life to pay for our sins. But He not only paid for our sins. He also paid for the sins of the whole world."

NIV

John is not talking to the world here; he is speaking to the church. He tells us what to do about sin after becoming Christians. God knows we're human and that we'll make mistakes. He wants us to understand that He does not want us to fall and stay down. He does not want us to live with guilt, refuses to forgive ourselves or deny Him the opportunity to forgive us.

The word "sin" means we have missed the mark. We have all done that; it will not be the last time. John tells us to admit our sins. If we don't acknowledge or confess our sin, we can't ask God to forgive us, and then we're stuck living with that sin. But if we ask God for mercy, He is faithful and will forgive us. Not only that, but He also cleanses us from all unrighteousness. Righteousness means right standing with God, and if we don't have right standing with God, we can't boldly enter the throne room of God. Jesus is our advocate, our mediator. His blood pleads our case to God, and it's always crying out, "You are forgiven," because of what He did on the cross. We know we're not perfect. As the Bible says, our righteousness is like filthy rags, so we can't argue our case. Jesus said He would stand in the gap for us; as the scripture above says, He is blameless. Jesus is always faithful, even when we are not.

So, the next time you "fall off the horse," boldly saddle back up and keep riding—but try to avoid the rocks. They hurt!

Chapter Twenty-Two

Dônde está el baño? (Where is the Bathroom?)

It was the summer of 1997, and I spent a couple of months working with some missionaries in Tenancingo, Mexico. Four others and I were summer servants, helping the full-time missionaries with friendship evangelism and planning a big campaign at the end of the summer. Every Tuesday, the summer servants had the day off, and we took advantage of these days to sightsee.

One particular Tuesday, my roommate Katrina and I were supposed to meet Margaret and Charity in the town of Ville Guerrero, where they were staying. We planned to meet early that morning at the bus station and catch another bus to Taxco, the famous silver jewelry town, to sightsee and buy lots of souvenirs. Katrina and I arrived at the bus station with plenty of time to meet the others and catch the next bus to Taxco. But the bus came and went, and Margaret and Charity hadn't shown up yet. With no way to contact them, we decided to wait a little longer before getting too worried.

At that moment, we had another problem—Katrina really needed to use the bathroom. She dashed off to the bus station restroom, which was just an outhouse, but she couldn't bring herself to use it. The smell was unbearable. She tried to hold her nose and go back in, but she still couldn't manage it and came back gagging. We brainstormed about where we could go that might have a decent restroom, but we didn't want to separate. We always tried not to go anywhere alone, and we didn't want to leave together and miss Margaret and Charity. Finally, the two of them arrived, apologizing for being late. Their host family had made them a big breakfast, and they felt they couldn't just eat and run. Katrina wasn't feeling too sympathetic because she had her own pressing issue.

The next bus to Taxco wasn't leaving for another hour, and Katrina couldn't wait that long. Even if we did wait, the bus ride was about two hours, and she wouldn't make it. So, we decided to take a cab for the hour-and-a-half trip to Taxco. We went to the taxi stand, where several drivers were bidding for our business. Katrina made the decision that we'd go with the one who could provide a clean restroom. In Mexico, businesses don't have to provide public restrooms, so it wasn't easy to find one. We ended up paying for Katrina to use a private restroom, and then we finally got on our way to Taxco.

Although the day started out a little chaotic, we ended up having a fantastic time. We shopped until we dropped, enjoyed a terrific meal, and took the bus back that evening. Life doesn't always go as planned, but I've learned that things often turn out better than expected with a little patience.

Life Insight: Good Overcomes Evil

> *"And we know that all things work together for good to them that love God, to them who are called according to His purpose."*
>
> Romans 8:28, KJV

How often have things happened in your life that you can't understand how they could work out? Romans tells us that we should know that God works everything out, no matter the problems. The reason we should know is because it is in His Word. To know means to learn by instruction, so if we are in the Word and learning His Word, then we should know. Faith comes by hearing and hearing by the Word of God, so hearing His Word teaches us to believe and know that He is faithful.

If you notice in the verse above, this promise in Romans is only given to those who love God, to those of us who have chosen to follow Him and obey Him. John 14:21 (NIV) says,

> *"Whoever has my commands and obeys them, he is the one who loves me. He who loves me will be loved by my Father, and I too will love him and show myself to him."*
>
> NKJV

This promise also applies to those who are called according to God's purpose—that is, those who have heard the call and accepted it.

There is a man who chose to believe in God and follow His purpose, and his name was Joseph. Joseph was a dreamer; you can find his story in the Book of Genesis. Joseph's brothers were jealous of him and sold him into slavery. This story is an excellent example of all things working together for good. Joseph wasn't just sold into slavery; he was also thrown into prison under pretenses. Yet, he stayed true to his beliefs and dreams. His faith in God and God's promises helped Joseph rise to the top. As he told his brothers in Genesis 50:20 (NLT), "Even though you planned evil against me, God planned good to come out of it. This was to keep many people alive, as He is doing now."

We must learn to trust God and, when things seem bleak, to look circumstances in the face and say, "God means it for good." When Satan comes knocking, let him know that through God, you will overcome. Even if it's as simple as overcoming all odds to find a clean restroom, we can overcome it.

Chapter Twenty-Three

What's that Smell?

My first trip to Haiti was a bit of an adventure—and by "adventure," I mean I had no clue what to expect. All I knew was that we were in for ten days of something, and I'd packed accordingly... or so I thought. We touched down, grabbed our bags, and then—bam!—as soon as we stepped outside the airport, we were swarmed by people offering to carry our bags for money or just outright begging. We barely squeezed through the crowd to our ride, waiting to be taken to the house where we'd stay in Port-au-Prince.

The first thing I noticed? The heat. I knew Haiti would be hot, but this was a whole new level. That first night was a special kind of miserable, and with no running water in the house, I couldn't even take a shower the next morning to freshen up. The next day, we boarded a tiny single-engine plane to the mountains. It was still hot, but the altitude made it bearable. The shade was our best friend, though finding a moment of privacy was another story. The sweet locals always wanted to be around us, which was endearing—until you just needed a minute alone. Returning to our room didn't help; we lost the breeze and were right back sweating.

And about that running water—at the mission, there wasn't any. Our water supply came straight from the river. When it was time to wash up, the local women would heat some of that river water, and we'd head to the "bathroom." Now, I use the term "bathroom" loosely—it was a dark little room with a drain through the wall and a basin filled with heated water and some soap. My bath routine involved a cup, some scooping, and a lot of prayers that I didn't get soap in my precious water source. Spoiler alert: I did and had to beg for more water, which was ice-cold because they hadn't had time to heat it. I'd feel clean and refreshed for all of five minutes before the sweat kicked in again. By the end of our ten days, I was thoroughly grossed out by myself, but hey, it was all worth it.

Before I knew it, our time was up, and we were on a plane headed to Miami. Let me tell you that air conditioning felt like heaven. As soon as we cleared customs, we made a beeline for Burger King. That was the best burger of my life—though, after ten days of beans, rice, and the occasional goat meat, anything would have tasted like gourmet cuisine.

Finally, it was time to board our flight home. I ended up sitting alone, away from the team, in a window seat. That's when I realized something terrible: I smelled. I mean, really smelled—like a delightful blend of body odor and the scents of Haiti. As I was pondering my odor dilemma, two very stylish women in expensive business suits sat down beside me, with flawless makeup and perfect hair. Meanwhile, I was a hot mess, and I knew it. The woman next to me smiled and asked how I was doing. I jumped at the chance to explain, "I'm so sorry, I know I don't smell great. I just spent ten days in Haiti on a mission trip and haven't had a proper bath..." I kept going, and she just smiled and said she understood.

Lesson learned. I pack my going-home outfit on every trip since in one of those fancy airtight bags. I don't break the seal until I'm at the airport. I head to the bathroom, give myself the best washcloth-and-soap bath I can manage, spritz on some body spray, fix my hair, and slap on some makeup. Never again will anyone sit next to me thinking, "What is that smell?"

Life Insight: Sweet-Smelling Aroma

Did you know that God has a sense of smell? Yep, it's true! The Bible mentions several things that God loves to smell—and some that He doesn't. Throughout the Old Testament, you'll find references to burnt offerings, described as a sweet-smelling aroma to Him. These offerings were more than smoke; they were acts of worship and thanksgiving.

Then there's this beautiful moment in Matthew 26:6-26, where a woman comes to Jesus with an alabaster jar of super expensive perfume. She anoints Him with it as an act of worship and sacrifice. The disciples weren't thrilled—they thought it was a waste and said it could've been sold to help the poor. But Jesus quickly set them straight: "She has done a beautiful thing to me." She wasn't wasting; she was pouring her praise on Him.

Fast forward to 2 Corinthians 2:14-15, where Paul says,

> "Thanks be to God, who always leads us in triumphal procession in Christ and through us spreads everywhere the fragrance of the knowledge of Him. For we are to God the aroma of Christ among those who are being saved."
>
> NIV

In other words, it's our job to spread the sweet aroma of Christ everywhere we go so that He can be known. Ephesians 5:1-2 backs this up by saying,

> *"Be imitators of God, therefore, as dearly loved children and live a life of love, just as Christ loved us and gave Himself up for us as a fragrant offering and sacrifice to God."*
>
> NIV

But how do we become this aroma of Christ? It's all about giving of ourselves. Whether it's our time, money, prayers, or even just being a witness to someone, each little act is a sacrifice of praise and worship to Him. So, spend time with Him, get to know Him, and prepare yourself to be used by Him. Just like Esther spent a year soaking in perfumes and oils to spend just a few minutes in the king's presence, we can do no less for the King of Kings. Present your bodies as a living sacrifice and get busy spreading the sweet aroma of our King—even if that smell happens to have a hint of Haiti in it. It's all good to Him!

Chapter Twenty-Four

Rest of the Story

Okay, you read about my horse fiasco; I had taken a not-so-graceful tumble off the horse and landed flat on my back. Ouch, right? But I never told you about what happened after, it was the most humbling experience I have ever had. After I had walked back to the mission, instead of getting back on the horse, I was already starting to feel sore; I had landed on my back pretty hard.

Sweet Nadish, our all-around saint who had been taking care of us all week: cleaning, cooking, and leading worship in the evenings like nobody's business, whisks me away to my room to take care of me. Nadish's care went beyond mere physical assistance; a profound expression of love and compassion touched me deeply. Her actions were accompanied by a sense of tenderness and genuine concern for my well-being as she tended to my soreness. First, by gently washing my feet, Nadish demonstrated hospitality and humility. In many cultures, washing someone's feet symbolizes servitude and respect, reflecting Jesus' act of humility in washing his disciples' feet. Nadish's willingness to perform this humble task showed her deep empathy and desire to alleviate my discomfort. Next, as she washed my back and began to massage me, Nadish's touch was soothing and comforting, as nice as any 5-star spa. Her hands moved with care and skill, easing the tension in my muscles and relieving the pain from my rough-and-tumble rodeo. But more than just physical relief, her massage conveyed a sense of emotional support and solidarity, reminding me that I was not alone in my struggles. Nadish's presence was a source of solace and reassurance during a moment of vulnerability.

But here's the kicker: I'm trying to shoo her away, feeling about as worthy of this royal treatment as a potato in a gourmet kitchen. I came here to minister to them, not end up on the receiving end of her ministering to me. But Nadish is not having any of my protests. She keeps on with her magic touch, and eventually, I surrender to the pampering.

I woke up early the next morning to the "morning prayer call" (see the chapter "Wake up Call"). As I mulled over the previous day's events, I felt a mix of embarrassment and gratitude. It turns out that even in my most clumsy moments, I can still be a poster child for Jesus, spreading His love and soaking up a bit of it myself.

As I lay there, replaying the scene from the night before and feeling like a total klutz, I can not help but think of Nadish and her quiet strength. Her kindness and compassion spoke volumes, reminding me it is okay to accept a helping hand now and then, even if I do not deserve it.

In the grand scheme, Nadish's care was more than just a spa day for my sore muscles. It was a living, breathing example of what it means to walk the Christian walk, showing me firsthand the power of lending a hand (or a massage) when someone is down and out. She was not just a caretaker but a walking, talking embodiment of God's love in action, turning a horse mishap into a lesson in grace and humility. And for that, I will forever be grateful.

Life Insight: Give and Take

The story of Nadish's care for me resonates deeply with the biblical accounts of Jesus' ministry, particularly in John 12:2-8 and John 13:1-5.

In John 12:2-8, we see Jesus being anointed by Mary with costly perfume. Initially, Judas criticizes Mary for her extravagance, questioning why the perfume wasn't sold and why money was given to the poor. However, Jesus defends Mary's actions, acknowledging the significance of her gesture. He states, "Leave her alone... She has done a beautiful thing to me." This story challenges our understanding of ministry by highlighting the importance of receiving acts of service and love from others. Just as Mary ministered to Jesus through her anointing, Nadish ministered to me through her care, demonstrating that ministry is not just about giving but also about receiving.

Similarly, in John 13:1-5, Jesus washes his disciples' feet, modeling humility and servanthood. Despite being their teacher and Lord, Jesus takes on the role of a servant, performing an act reserved for the lowest of servants. Peter initially objects, but Jesus explains that he has no part with him unless he washes Peter's feet. This foot-washing symbolizes Jesus' sacrificial love and is a powerful example of humble service.

Nadish's actions echo this spirit of humble service, as she tended to my needs with kindness and compassion, embodying the selfless love of Christ. In reflecting on these biblical stories alongside my own experience, I realized that true ministry encompasses both giving and receiving. Just as Jesus allowed himself to be ministered to by Mary and demonstrated humble service to his disciples, so too should we be open to both giving and receiving care within the Christian community. Nadish's care for me challenged my pride and self-sufficiency, reminding me of humanity's interconnectedness and reliance on each other. Ultimately, this experience deepened my understanding of the true nature of service and humility, emphasizing the importance of giving and receiving love in the faith journey.

Chapter Twenty-Five

Just One Coffee

My Uncle Kermit and I were on a train platform in Germany, patiently waiting for our train. There was a coffee kiosk in the middle of the platform, and my uncle decided he wanted a coffee. He went up to the kiosk, and an older lady was there, ready to take his order.

My uncle isn't exactly fluent in German, so he uses the classic "one coffee" line with the universal index finger point to hopefully bridge any language gaps. But, oh boy, did things take a turn.

She looked at him sternly and asked, "One coffee or two?" As she asked, she would hold up her thumb and then her index finger. Confused, my uncle told her again, "One coffee," as he held up his index finger. Very irritably, she asked again, "One coffee or two?" She again held up her thumb and then index finger as she repeated the question.

Bless his soul, Uncle Kermit is now confused as a chameleon in a bag of Skittles. He insists once more, "Just one coffee," with an even more determined finger-point. The lady then looked at my uncle for a moment and then held up her thumb. "In Germany, when you hold up a thumb, that is one, and if you hold up a finger, that means two," she explained while glaring at him.

At this point, I'm losing it. Here are these two, locked in a battle of coffee wits, and I'm half expecting them to break out into a full-on barista brawl. My money's on the German lady—she had that look like she's seen a latte more than a few showdowns.

But lo and behold, Uncle Kermit, takes a breath, swallows his pride (and possibly a few choice words) and holds up his thumb like he's signaling for a cab. "One coffee," he says, with a grin that could charm the caffeine out of a bean.

And just like that, peace is restored between America and Germany—all thanks to a little misunderstanding over a cup of joe. Ah, the things you encounter on a train platform—it's a wild world out there, folks!

Life Insights: Cultural Differences

One of my childhood pastors was passionate about overseas ministry, bringing the Gospel to diverse cultures. He imparted valuable advice for those traveling to minister in new countries: "Stop at the border and learn what the sins are to them." Cultural perceptions of sin vary widely; for instance, while some cultures may view coffee as sinful, others may not consider alcohol as such. This underscores the importance of understanding and respecting cultural differences, as exemplified in my experience with coffee.

This lesson was evident during our mission trip to Haiti. In Haitian churches, women traditionally cover their heads. Although this practice wasn't customary for me or my church team, we respectfully wore scarves in church to avoid offending.

The debate over whether women should cover their heads in the church often references 1 Corinthians 11:6, which suggests that women who don't cover their heads might as well shave them.

> *"For if a woman does not cover her head, she might as well have her hair cut off; but if it is a disgrace for a woman to have her hair cut off or her head shaved, then she should cover her head."*
>
> NIV

However, interpretations vary. Some argue that long hair is a sufficient covering, as stated in 1 Corinthians 11:15,

> *"But that if a woman has long hair, it is her glory? For long hair is given to her as a covering."*
>
> NASB

I view such debates as legalistic distractions from the grace of God, who is our ultimate covering through Jesus Christ.

In Romans 4:6-8, the Apostle Paul illustrates this grace by likening it to the Passover lamb's blood, which covered the Israelites' homes and spared them from the angel of Death.

> *"just as David also describes the blessedness of the man to whom God imputes righteousness apart from works:* "Blessed are those whose **lawless deeds are forgiven**, **And whose sins are covered**; Blessed is the man to whom the **Lord shall not impute sin**."
>
> NKJV, emphasis mine

The blood of Jesus cleanses us from ALL sin. This is not just salvation, but it is ongoing—for our past sins, our sins today, and our sins tomorrow.

During our Haiti trip, we witnessed the danger of religious legalism overshadowing the message of God's love and salvation. Despite our teachings on grace, an older woman's emphasis on enforcing head coverings during a salvation moment saddened me deeply. A young teenage girl came up for salvation, and as we were ministering to her, another woman threw a head covering for her to put on. Here, we have been teaching about God's love, mercy, and grace for us. That Jesus' blood was shed for our salvation, that He is our final sacrifice, and to that older woman in the church, what was important to her was that this young girl covers her head, not that she receives salvation. This incident highlighted the Pharisaical tendency to prioritize adherence to laws over embracing God's love and freedom.

In Matthew 5:17, Jesus affirms that He came not to abolish the Law but to fulfill it, emphasizing love as the fulfillment of the law. Consequently, I chose not to wear a head covering during the remainder of our trip, striving to convey the message that God's love transcends legalistic practices.

In essence, Jesus embodies love. His message emphasizes liberation from legalism, inviting all to experience God's boundless grace and love.

In conclusion, as we continue to spread God's love and grace, let's remain mindful of cultural differences. Just as my pastor advised us to understand the unique perspectives on sin at each border, we should also approach ministry with sensitivity and respect for diverse cultural practices. By doing so, we can effectively convey the universal message of God's love while honoring the rich tapestry of cultural traditions worldwide. But don't let it overshadow God's grace and mercy or let legalism steal someone's joy.

CHAPTER TWENTY-SIX

When the Journey Leaves a Mark

"We are hard pressed on every side, but not crushed; perplexed, but not in despair; persecuted, but not abandoned; struck down, but not destroyed."

2 Corinthians 4:8-9, NIV

Rome. A city of ancient wonders, where history is layered beneath every step. I marveled at the Colosseum, navigated its overcrowded trains (once was enough), and found refreshment in the cool, crisp water from ancient fountains. But as I explored Palatine Hill, ruins scattered everywhere, I tripped over a rock—or maybe a piece of history—and twisted my ankle.

Determined not to let it ruin my trip, I wrapped my ankle and pressed on. Every night, I cut away the bandages and dealt with the swelling, refusing to slow down. When I finally got home, my doctor said I would have been better off breaking it—because then I would have stopped and let it heal. Instead, I had done more damage, requiring nine months in a boot and six months of therapy. Even now, I still feel the effects of that choice.

Oddly enough, Rome's underground subway system tells a similar story. Unlike other major cities, Rome's metro is small because every time they try to expand, they run into history—ancient ruins buried just beneath the surface. Progress halts, archaeologists step in, and preservation takes priority. It's frustrating, but necessary.

How often do we try to push forward in life, only to stumble over something God wants us to deal with? We want to move faster, to get to where we think we need to be, but sometimes God allows us to uncover hidden things that need our attention—wounds, struggles, or lessons we have yet to learn. Instead of viewing these moments as setbacks, what if we saw them as God's way of preserving something valuable in us?

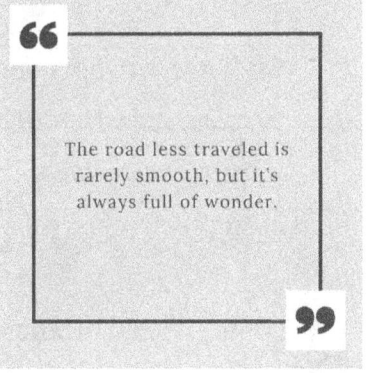

> The road less traveled is rarely smooth, but it's always full of wonder.

I thought I was showing strength by pushing through my injury, but real strength would have been knowing when to stop and heal.

Maybe that is what God is asking of you today—not to press on at all costs, but to pause, reflect, and let Him work in the places you would rather ignore.

Life Insight: Learning When to Push Through and When to Pause

Sometimes, determination is our greatest strength—but it can also be our downfall. There's a fine line between perseverance and stubbornness, and learning when to push forward and when to rest is a mark of wisdom.

In life, we all face moments where we trip over something unexpected—whether it's a challenge, a setback, or even our own pride. The temptation is to press on at all costs, fearing that slowing down means giving up. But just like my ankle in Rome, pushing through without proper healing can cause more damage in the long run.

The same is true in our spiritual journey. There are seasons to fight, to endure, and to run the race. But there are also seasons where God calls us to rest, to heal, and to allow Him to do the work we cannot do on our own. Ignoring those moments can lead to deeper wounds, prolonged struggles, and scars that take longer to heal.

Take a moment today to pause and reflect. Is there an area of your life where you've been pushing through, ignoring the need for healing? Ask God for the wisdom to recognize when it's time to rest and let

Him restore you. Embrace the healing He offers and trust that He will guide you to the next step in His perfect timing.

Chapter Twenty-Seven

Lost and Found

Melanie and I were on a four-day cruise from Charleston, South Carolina, to the Bahamas, joined by her parents—my Aunt Sue and Uncle Vann. It was the perfect getaway, a chance to unwind, soak in the sunshine, and do a whole lot of nothing. And let me tell you, we took that mission seriously. The adults-only deck became our happy place, complete with a pool, endless ocean views, and just the right amount of relaxation. At lunch, we discovered a little hidden gem—a quiet bar with the best empanadas, which quickly became our daily tradition.

Everything was going great until Melanie realized her cell phone was missing. That would have been bad enough, but this wasn't just any cell phone—it had her wallet attached, holding her credit cards and driver's license. And of course, the same credit card she was using to pay for everything on the cruise. The realization sent a jolt through us. Losing a phone is stressful anywhere, but on a floating city in the middle of the ocean? That felt next-level.

Panic could have easily set in, but before we did anything else, we stopped and prayed. We asked God to keep her phone and all its contents safe and to help us find it. Then, we got to work. We retraced her steps, checked every place she had been, and made multiple trips to the service desk, but nothing. No phone. No wallet. No credit cards. No ID. It was enough to make anyone anxious, but Melanie kept saying she felt at peace.

Now, I'm not saying she wasn't concerned. I mean, it's hard not to think about worst-case scenarios when your identity and finances are literally floating somewhere on the open seas. But deep down, she knew—we knew—God was in control. The next morning, still hopeful but understandably a bit worried, Melanie went to check with the service desk one more time. And there it was. Found overnight by the cleaning crew in one of the public restrooms. Everything inside, untouched.

Life Insight: Trusting God in the Waiting

"You will keep in perfect peace those whose minds are steadfast, because they trust in you."
Isaiah 26:3, NIV

This verse isn't just a comforting promise; it's a spiritual principle. Perfect peace isn't the absence of trouble—it's the presence of trust. The Hebrew word for "perfect peace" here is *shalom shalom*, meaning a deep, unshakable wholeness that remains steady no matter the circumstances. It doesn't mean life will always be smooth sailing, but it does mean we can remain anchored, even when storms arise.

Melanie experienced this firsthand. Even after praying, she could have let fear take over, running every worst-case scenario through her mind. But instead, she clung to that sense of peace, knowing God was in control. That is what it means to have a steadfast mind—one that isn't tossed around by worry but is fixed on God's faithfulness.

So often, we pray and then immediately pick our burdens back up, acting as if God needs our help to figure things out. But real trust looks like resting in Him even when the solution hasn't shown up yet. His peace isn't dependent on the outcome; it's dependent on our faith in the One who holds the outcome.

If you are waiting for an answer, a breakthrough, or a resolution, ask yourself: Is my mind steadfast, or am I letting fear and doubt take over? God's peace is available, but it comes when we fix our thoughts on Him, not on the problem. Just like Melanie's phone was never truly lost—God knew exactly where it was the entire time—your situation isn't out of His hands. He is already at work. You can rest in that.

Chapter Twenty-Eight

Island Odyssey: A Golf Cart Adventure

During a memorable cruise escapade alongside two of my closest pals, our ship docked on the scenic shores of Grand Turk Island. Uncertain about our plans due to the recent havoc wreaked by a devastating hurricane, we deliberated over our options. Despite the island's recent trials, we unanimously agreed to veer off the beaten path and forge our own adventure, foregoing the usual ship-sponsored excursions.

Deciding to embrace some spontaneity, we rented a gas-powered golf cart to explore the island's 7-mile stretch. I ended up driving, trying to navigate both the unfamiliar terrain and the British custom of driving on the left side of the road. Things were going fine—until we hit a roundabout. I froze, unsure of what to do, and made the ultimate roundabout mistake: stopping.

Two cars approached, and I awkwardly gestured, admitting my confusion. To my relief (and embarrassment), they kindly stopped and waved me through. Laughing at my rookie mistake, we waved back, probably solidifying their impression of us as adventurous but clueless Americans.

Despite the comical mishap, our day unfolded into an unforgettable odyssey, brimming with laughter and discovery. We embarked on a leisurely exploration, stopping intermittently to marvel at the island's wonders. From the iconic lighthouse to engaging conversations with locals, each moment we have added to the tapestry of our adventure. Stumbling upon a secluded beach adorned with graceful flamingos, we reveled in the moment's tranquility before indulging in delectable conch fritters, a culinary delight unique to the island.

Our journey led us past the Salinas, natural saltwater depressions once vital to the island's salt production. Amidst the tranquil landscape, we encountered remnants of a bygone era, including horses and donkeys that once toiled in the saltworks. A near-miss with a wandering horse was a poignant reminder to remain vigilant, a lesson learned amidst the island's untamed beauty. "I swear I didn't see him, officer!"

As our escapade drew close, we reluctantly returned our trusty golf cart, exchanging tales of our exploits with fellow cruisers. With hearts brimming with exhilaration, we regaled them with our escapades, confident that our impromptu adventure trumped any prepackaged excursion. With memories etched in our minds, we bid adieu to

Grand Turk Island, cherishing the bonds forged and the unforgettable moments shared amidst its sun-kissed shores.

Life Insight: Unexpected Perspective

As we embarked on our golf cart adventure, we were reminded of the transformative power of renewing our perspectives, a concept echoed in Romans 12:2.

> *"Do not conform to the pattern of this world but be transformed by the renewing of your mind. Then you will be able to test and approve what God's will is – his good, pleasing and perfect will."*
>
> NIV

Riding around the island, you could not avoid the destruction that the hurricane left in its wake. But talking with the islanders, you realize that their resilience was nothing short of remarkable. Homes were reduced to rubble, streets were littered with debris, and the landscape bore the scars of nature's fury. Yet, amidst the chaos and devastation, a spirit of determination and perseverance emerged.

Romans 12:2 reminds us not to conform to the patterns of this world but to be transformed by the renewing of our minds. In the face of adversity, the islanders exemplified this transformative mindset. Instead of succumbing to despair or resignation, they chose to rise above the devastation, embracing a renewed sense of purpose and hope.

The process of rebuilding after the hurricane was not merely a physical endeavor but a spiritual and emotional journey as well. It required a shift in mindset—a conscious decision to reject defeatism and embrace a vision of restoration and renewal. This transformation of the mind enabled the islanders to tap into their inner strength and resilience, empowering them to rebuild their lives and communities from the ground up.

As we reflect on Romans 12:2 in the context of the hurricane and the subsequent rebuilding efforts, we are reminded of the power of faith and perseverance in the face of adversity. Just as the islanders refused to conform to the despair and destruction around them, we, too, are called to resist the negative influences of the world and instead allow our minds to be transformed by the truth and promises of God's word.

By renewing our minds, we gain clarity of vision and discernment of God's will for our lives. We can see beyond the immediate challenges and obstacles, trusting that God's plan is good, pleasing, and perfect. Like the islanders of Grand Turk, may we be strengthened and transformed by renewing our minds as we press forward in faith, hope, and perseverance.

Chapter Twenty-Nine

Traveling Light

I'll never forget my first mission trip. It was to Mexico for a week, and to say I was clueless would be an understatement. I had no idea what we'd be doing, what the weather was like, or even how the locals dressed. So, naturally, I over-prepared. And by over-prepared, I mean I brought two enormous bags stuffed to the brim. The guys took one look at my luggage and made it clear: I was on my own. If I brought it, I could carry it. Spoiler alert: I didn't even use half of what I packed, but hey, at least I had options, right?

A few years later, I embarked on a two-and-a-half-month mission trip back to Mexico. You'd think I would've learned my lesson, but nope. This time, I hauled a gigantic duffel bag with wheels. I figured, "It has wheels—how hard could it be?" So, naturally, I stuffed it with everything I could think of. I was going to be there all summer, and I had no clue what I'd need.

As if the overpacking wasn't enough, I bought even more stuff while there—clothes, gifts, souvenirs, jewelry, a blanket, and even a pot. By the end of the summer, my bag was practically bursting at the seams, held together by a generous amount of duct tape. (Duct tape really is a miracle worker, isn't it?) But could I leave anything behind? Of course not! I couldn't bring myself to part with a single item, so I struggled with my mountain of luggage all by myself.

Over the years, I've learned some valuable lessons: simplify and let go. Now, I can head to Haiti for a week or two with nothing more than a backpack. And let me tell you, the relief of leaving all that extra weight behind is incredible. I once heard a pretty savvy traveler say, "You'll never go on a trip and come back thinking, 'Next time, I'll pack more.'" And they were absolutely right.

Life Insight: Weightless

Over the years, we all have collected a little (or a lot) of emotional baggage. Life can throw some pretty tough stuff our way, and the stress and pain we experience can feel like an extra hundred pounds weighing us down. You know the baggage I'm talking about—the kind that clutters your mind and heart, making everything feel heavier than it should. But here's the good news: God's got a much better plan for us. He invites us to exchange our heavy loads for His peace. In Matthew 11:29-30, Jesus says,

> *"Take my yoke upon you, and learn from me, for I am gentle and humble in heart, and you will find rest for your souls. For my yoke is easy and my burden is light."*
>
> KJV

Now, let's unpack that a bit. In Jesus' time, a yoke was a wooden frame used to pair two oxen together, allowing them to share the load as they plowed a field. When Jesus says, *"Take my yoke upon you,"* He's inviting us to be yoked with Him, to share our burdens with Him. But here's the twist—Jesus isn't offering us just any yoke. His yoke is easy, and His burden is light. He's not here to add more weight to our already heavy hearts. Instead, He wants to lighten our load by walking alongside us, guiding us, and giving us the strength to keep going.

And when He says, *"Learn from me, for I am gentle and humble in heart,"* He's reassuring us that He's not harsh or demanding. He's gentle, understanding, and full of compassion. Jesus knows exactly what we're going through because He's been there. He's walked this earth, faced the struggles we face, and experienced the pain we feel. That's why He can offer us proper rest—not just physical rest, but deep, soul-level rest that refreshes our spirits and brings us peace.

It took me a long time to grasp this. Like many, I would try to give my burdens to God, only to snatch them back as soon as things got tough. I had to learn to trust the Lord enough to leave my worries in His hands over time, and maybe you can relate. But here's the thing—Jesus knows what it's like to carry the weight of the world on His shoulders. He took on that burden so we wouldn't have to.

He's not asking us to struggle under the load of our worries, guilt, or brokenness. Instead, He's inviting us to let go of that weight and allow Him to carry it for us. Imagine Him saying, "You look worn out. Let Me take that heavy load off your shoulders. It looks like it's been weighing you down for too long. Let Me hold your hand and walk with you—I promise I'll never leave your side." And when He takes our burdens, He doesn't replace them with more weight. Instead, He fills us with love, peace, comfort, and forgiveness.

So, the next time you feel overwhelmed by life's burdens, remember that Jesus is ready and willing to carry them for you. He's got your back and Offers you a lighter, easier path to walk—one filled with His grace and peace.

Chapter Thirty

Fill 'er Up

In 2007, I worked on a bank's New Branch Opening Team—a job I truly enjoyed. My partner, Mike, and I were responsible for setting up new branches, training employees, and pre-marketing for about four weeks before each branch opened. Once the branch was up and running, we'd move on to the next location. Occasionally, we'd attend grand openings at other branches to lend a helping hand.

One Saturday, we helped open a branch two hours from our current location. After celebrating the successful launch with the team over dinner, Mike and I decided to stay overnight and drive back the next morning.

The drive on Sunday started quietly. We were both tired from the weekend's festivities, so we relaxed, listened to music, and didn't talk much. But about 40 minutes into our drive, we noticed a problem—Mike's truck was running low on gas.

His truck had one of those handy dashboards that displayed the exact miles left until empty. At first, we weren't worried. We spotted a gas station up ahead but decided to pass it by. It was owned by a company associated with the controversial Hugo Chavez from Venezuela, and we didn't feel right fueling up there. I mean, the man hated America and all we stand for, so we were showing our American Pride and not giving him any of our money! No problem, we thought—another station would be along shortly.

As we drove on, my cousin Melanie called. We chatted and laughed while Mike looked for another station. We passed a second one—the same ownership—and kept driving. I glanced over at Mike; he didn't seem nervous, so I was not worried either.

Then a third station appeared—again, the same. Now, the truck's countdown showed seven miles until empty. Mike's calm demeanor began to crack. "Get off the phone; we're going to run out of gas!" he said urgently.

I told Melanie I would call her later and hung up, and Mike quickly started programming his GPS to locate the nearest gas station. The countdown dropped to three miles. Then two. Then one. Finally, the dreaded *zero*.

We were coasting on fumes, praying we'd reach a station. With the air conditioning off and windows down to save every ounce of fuel, we nervously eyed each hill, convinced the incline would be our undoing.

But by some miracle—literally—we rolled into a gas station just as the truck was about to give up. And thankfully, it wasn't one we had sworn off.

As we filled the tank, the tension broke, and we laughed. I teased Mike about how panicked he had been. "Why did you want me off the phone so badly? There wasn't anything I could do!" I asked.

He chuckled and admitted, "I just needed you to panic with me. That's what partners are for, right?"

Life Insight: He Provides

When life's tank is running low—gas, energy, or patience—it's all too easy to spiral into panic mode. You know the feeling: the gas light is blinking, the kids are arguing in the back seat, and you're seriously considering that last cupcake as emotional support. But Psalm 23 swoops in like a divine roadside assistance plan, reminding us that the Lord is our Shepherd—who cares for us, leads us, and provides for every need.

> *"The Lord is my shepherd; I lack nothing. He makes me lie down in green pastures, he leads me beside quiet waters, he refreshes my soul."*
>
> Psalm 23:1-3, NIV

Just like a shepherd making sure the sheep are fed, watered, and not wandering off cliffs, God promises that when we follow His lead, we'll lack nothing.

Take it from me—I've been there, white-knuckling the steering wheel as the gas gauge hit "E" and debating whether coasting down hill counts as fuel conservation. But as soon as we paused the panic and prayed, God led us to a gas station just in time. He knew our need before we even muttered, "Lord, help." It's funny how He often waits for us to stop flailing and start trusting.

So, the next time you're running on empty—whether it's your car, your energy, or your patience—remember this: the Shepherd is always on duty. He'll lead you to green pastures (or at least a parking spot), quiet waters (or a moment of peace), and exactly what you need when you need it. Trust Him—He's got your back...and your gas tank.

Chapter Thirty-One

When Silence Speaks

Many years ago, my "nephew" Alex (nephew by love, not blood) wanted to join the Cub Scouts. Sounds simple enough, right? Sign a few papers, buy a uniform, and off he goes.

Except, his father had just passed away. And I made up my mind, I was going to see to it that Alex got this opportunity. He needed it.

It just so happened that my cousin Vann was the Cub Scout Master. Perfect, I thought. He'd look out for Alex, and I wouldn't have to worry.

So, I showed up ready to sign Alex up. I even asked Vann if he needed any help. In my mind, "help" meant maybe snacks, or organizing paperwork, or keeping up with carpool schedules. Easy stuff.

Vann grinned and said, "Yes, I could use some help." Then he handed me a thick Leader's Book for the Wolf Den.

I blinked at it. "What is this?"

He laughed. "Welcome to Pack 25. You're our newest Pack Leader."

And just like that, I was drafted.

I had no idea what I was in for. Years of Cub Scout meetings. Camping trips. Den projects. And little boys proudly bringing me frogs and lizards, shoving them inches from my face. (Rule #1: never, ever show fear when an 8-year-old is dangling a reptile in your direction.)

But you know what? I ended up loving it. Every muddy, frog-filled, campfire-smoky minute of it.

A few years later, Vann did it again. He "voluntold" me. This time, he said he needed a female leader for the Venturing crew. And oh, by the way, we were going sailing around the Florida Keys for ten days.

I mean, twist my arm why don't you. Ten days on a sailboat? Sure, I guess I could endure that. The only catch? Six teenagers came with the deal. (Just kidding—they were a blast.)

So off we went. Two cars. Two adults. Six teenagers. Destination: Florida Boy Scouts Sea Base in Islamorada.

When we arrived, we boarded the sailboat that would be our home. It had two small cabins—one for the captain, and one up front with a couple of bunks that Vann and I shared. The kids spread out wherever they could. Some claimed benches in the galley. A few braved the floor. Most chose the deck under the stars, which honestly was the smartest choice. Cooler air, better view.

The most interesting part of the trip wasn't the snorkeling, or the sailing, or even the kids trying to cook on a tiny boat stove. It was *night watch.*

Every night, someone had to stay awake for an hour. The job was simple: make sure the boat didn't drift by checking the anchor, and keep an eye on the lights. When your hour was up, you woke the next person.

One night, it was my turn. Everyone else was sound asleep. The water was calm. Still, like glass. Not a ripple. Not even a breeze. Which made it hot and sticky in the Florida humidity, but strangely peaceful.

It felt a little eerie—just me, the stars, and the sound of silence. But it was also beautiful.

My hour passed. I should have gone below to wake up the next watch. But I didn't. I sat there another hour, just breathing it all in. The stillness. The quiet. The feeling that time had slowed to a crawl. It was one of those rare moments where peace outweighed everything else.

Life Insight: God in the Quiet Hours

That night on the boat taught me something.

Sometimes God calls us to "night watch." To sit still. To stay awake when the world around us is asleep. To hold steady, even when nothing seems to be happening.

We don't always like it. We prefer movement, action, and results. But the stillness has a purpose. It's in the stillness that you learn to listen.

Psalm 46:10 says,

> *"Be still, and know that I am God."*
>
> KJV

That verse doesn't mean doing nothing. It means trusting that God is holding things together when you can't see movement. It means staying faithful in the quiet hours, knowing He hasn't forgotten you.

The night watch isn't wasted. It's where peace takes root. It's where you realize you don't have to control everything—you just have to stay present and trust Him.

So let me ask you: what "night watch" season are you in? Where is God asking you to stay awake, stay faithful, and trust Him—even when the waters look still?

The peace you long for may not come in the daylight rush. It may come in the quiet hour, when it's just you, the stars, and the steady presence of God.

Chapter Thirty-Two

The Sweetest Vacation

Back in 2017, Melanie and I planned a Spring Break trip to Hershey, Pennsylvania. But this time, we threw in a sweet little twist—we were *not* alone. Oh no, this was no quiet getaway for two. We loaded up my mom's faithful minivan with groceries, clothes, three guitars, three ukuleles, and five wide-eyed kids: my three nephews and Melanie's niece and nephew. Just imagine the *chaos* and giggles. We affectionately dubbed our traveling crew "The No Parents Tour." Technically, we were the adults... but let's be honest, we were just older kids with driver's licenses.

We rented a cozy cabin at the Hershey campground and made it our home base for a week of laughter, exploration, and unforgettable bonding. The boys took over the bunk room with two bunk beds, Melanie and I shared a double in the master bedroom, and sweet Shay claimed the couch with all the nobility of a queen exiled to the living room. But truly, the biggest challenge we faced? Sharing *one* bathroom. Seven people. One toilet. God bless us.

Day one kicked off with all the adrenaline Hersheypark could offer, where the youngest and smallest in our crew, Alex, discovered he was just tall enough to ride his very first roller coaster. His joy—and our cheers—made that moment one for the books.

The days that followed were a blur of chocolate, culture, and the kind of wonder that only childhood (and maybe a sugar rush) can bring. We rode an old-fashioned trolley through the town, learned about Milton Hershey's legacy (talk about a man who turned cocoa into a calling!), and created our own custom candy bars, complete with sprinkles, smiles, and sticky fingers.

We even dipped our toes into the peaceful rhythms of Amish country. Picture this: a horse-drawn buggy clip-clopping along a quiet road, fresh lemonade in hand—seriously, it was the best lemonade we've ever had, and I still dream about it—and kids marveling at how people could *live* without Wi-Fi. We capped off the day at a mini-golf and arcade spot that was clearly designed to drain wallets and fill hearts. Alex hit a jackpot and walked out with enough tickets to fill a backpack—and traded them in for a treasure trove of dollar-store toys that instantly became priceless.

But the evenings… oh, the evenings were where the real magic happened. After long days of exploring, we'd gather around the fire to roast s'mores, cook simple meals together, strum our instruments, and make up silly verses to campfire songs like a goofy little traveling band. We laughed until we cried. Told stories. Shared snacks and secrets. One night, a distant cousin—who saw our trip on social media—realized we were in town and showed up with a bag of marshmallows to join the fun. Only in our world does a Facebook post turn into a campfire reunion!

We even made time for a little soul nourishment. One day, we took the kids to Sight & Sound Theatre to see *Jonah*, and I will never forget the look of awe on their faces during the storm scenes—or the stillness in their hearts when Jonah finally surrendered to God's calling. It was powerful, moving, and the perfect reminder that God chases us with mercy, no matter where we try to hide.

But you know what? The sweetest part of the whole trip wasn't the chocolate—though trust me, we ate *plenty*. It was the memories. The connection. The late-night whispers and the sticky hands and the sound of five kids howling with laughter over who dropped their s'more in the fire (it was me). It was being fully present. Fully in the moment. Fully alive.

To this day, my nephews still say, "That was the best vacation we've ever had." And you know what? I agree. Not because it was fancy. Not because it was flawless. But because it was *real*. Love, laughter, and a whole lot of Hershey's chocolate.

Life Insight: Faith found in Chocolate and S'mores

The whole trip reminds me of Psalm 34:8:

> "Taste and see that the Lord is good; blessed is the one who takes refuge in Him."
>
> NIV

This wasn't just a memory-making vacation. It was a living, breathing picture of that verse in action.

You see, God's goodness isn't confined to stained glass windows or softly spoken prayers. It is not reserved for mountaintop moments or spiritual high points. No, His goodness often sneaks up on us in the *ordinary made sacred*—in the crackle of a campfire, the sound of children's laughter drifting through a cabin, the shared joy of an arcade jackpot, or a ukulele song made up on the spot.

We tasted that goodness—literally and spiritually. And I do not mean just the s'mores (though those were divine). I mean the flavor of fellowship. The sweetness of slowing down. The rich, full taste of being present, being known, being loved.

God's goodness is not just a concept to believe—it's an experience to savor.

Just like Alex had to stretch to meet the height requirement for his first roller coaster, sometimes we find ourselves needing to stretch spiritually. We may feel like we are not quite tall enough, brave enough, worthy enough—but God invites us to grow. And when we do? We find that the ride He has planned for us is *so much more exhilarating* than we imagined. It might be fast. It might turn unexpectedly. But oh, it is full of life.

Then there was our visit to *Sight & Sound Theatre,* where we sat wide-eyed watching the story of Jonah unfold before us. A prophet who tried to escape God's assignment—and yet was *relentlessly pursued* by mercy. Watching it with five kids, some just beginning to understand how big God's love is, was a reminder to me too: God's plan will always find us, no matter how far we drift or how deep we dive.

Even Jonah, in the belly of a fish, was not too far gone. That is the kind of God we serve. A God who doesn't just demand obedience, but invites us into redemption. A God who meets us in the detours, disciplines us in love, and still calls us worthy of the mission.

This wasn't just a trip—it was a sacred pause.

A time to remember that life with God is not just holy—it's *happy*. Joy-filled. Overflowing with giggles and grace. We roasted marshmallows, but God roasted our hearts in the best way—warming them, softening them, filling them with sweet reminders of His presence in the small things.

And just like Hershey's chocolate... once you've truly tasted God's goodness?
You crave it.
You chase it.
You want to invite others to try it too.

This trip was more than just a vacation. It was a holy reminder that life with God is rich, real, and full of joy. And just like Hershey's chocolate, once you've had a taste of His goodness, you'll always want more.

Chapter Thirty-Three
Stow Aways

My friend and I decided to seize the day and hopped on a last-minute cruise from Miami. Finding those leftover cabins for a steal was a stroke of luck, so we gunned it from Greensboro, NC, to Miami in record time. Man, were we beat when we finally rolled in, but we were pumped for our 4-day getaway. Mexico was our destination, with a beach bash on the agenda –picture us chilling in lounge chairs, sipping something cold, and soaking up the sun.

Little did we know, we stumbled onto a cruise packed with die-hard Pittsburgh Steeler fans. I'm talking seas of green and yellow everywhere you turn! No one warned us about that! Nearly everyone onboard was part of the Steeler nation, and let me tell you, they've got their own vibe. No offense, but we Southerners move at a different pace, a bit more laid-back. Still, it was a blast soaking up the atmosphere.

Day one was a dream. We plopped down by the pool and didn't budge all day. After a satisfying dinner, we hit the sack early, eager for beach adventures the next day. Our cabin might've been cozy, but those two big porthole windows gave us killer ocean views.

Things took an unexpected turn on the second morning. I woke up feeling off, and when I glanced out the porthole, I realized we were dead in the water. What in the world? I didn't have to wait too long to find out, but soon, there came an announcement from the bridge – a distress signal from a raft nearby. They didn't want to rattle the guests too early, but we were informed they were rescuing folks lost at sea. Peeking out, I spotted the raft, and my heart sank.

From my porthole, I saw the ship crew launch a lifeboat and slowly make its way to the raft. Turns out, it was a homemade contraption carrying around 60 Cuban migrants, stranded for days without food and water. The crew whisked them away below deck, tending to their needs. But the sad reality hit: once we hit port, they'd likely be handed over to the Mexican authorities, possibly facing a return to Cuba.

It broke my heart—these folks risked it all to escape their situation only to face uncertainty. And then you had passengers griping about canceled excursions because of the delay. Seriously, these are first-world problems, right?

Sure, our plans got nixed, too, but Jessica and I made the most of it. We found a beachside masseuse and treated ourselves to a blissful massage with the waves as our soundtrack. Then, a scrumptious Mexican dinner sealed the deal. It was a humbling reminder of just how fortunate we are. Every moment becomes a lesson in gratitude, a stark contrast to the struggles faced by those brave souls we encountered at sea.

Life Insight: Count Your Blessings

One of my favorite Christmas movies is "White Christmas." It's enchanting music and lively dance numbers transport me to a picturesque inn in Vermont, creating a sense of joy and nostalgia. One of my favorite scenes from the movie is when Rosemary Cloney's character could not sleep so she heads back to the lodge for a little food. She meets Bing Crosby's character and their encounter turns delightful when Crosby jokingly advises Clooney about the connection between sandwiches and dreams. The scene concludes with Crosby singing a tender lullaby that echoes the sentiment, *"When I'm worried and I can't sleep, I count my blessings instead of sheep, And I fall asleep counting my blessings..."*

This heartwarming moment is a gentle reminder to reflect on our lives. When was the last time you counted your blessings? Amidst the hustle and bustle, it's easy to get caught up in the challenges and concerns, losing sight of the abundant blessings surrounding us. Perhaps it's time for a shift in perspective, a moment to recognize that God is always ready to pour His blessings upon us.

2 Corinthians 9:8 says, *"God can pour on the blessings in astonishing ways so that you're ready for anything and everything, more than just ready to do what needs to be done."* (The Message Bible).

We are reminded that God's blessings can manifest in astonishing ways, preparing us for every challenge that comes our way. The Message Bible articulates it beautifully, emphasizing that we are not only blessed but blessed to be a blessing. God desires to meet our needs and provide abundantly so we can extend blessings to others.

If we listen to our God, he will rain blessings on us. Deuteronomy 28:2 says that his blessings chase you and overtake you. The chapter unfolds, outlining blessings in health, prosperity, and victory over adversaries. God desires to make us the head and not the tail, offering breakthroughs and treasures of goodness. Yet, a pivotal moment of choice is highlighted in Deuteronomy 28:1—an invitation contingent on our obedience to God's commands. *"Now it shall come to pass, if you diligently obey the voice of the Lord your God, to observe carefully all His commandments which I command you today..."*

See, I knew there was a catch, you might be thinking. Yep, you see, God set a choice in front of you. Deuteronomy 30:15:20,

> *"Look at what I've done for you today: I've placed in front of you Life and Good Death and Evil. And I command you today: Love God, your God. Walk in his ways. Keep his commandments, regulations, and rules so that you will live, really live, live exuberantly, blessed by God, your God, in the land you are about to enter and possess. But I warn you: If you have a change of heart, refuse to listen obediently, and willfully go off to serve and worship other*

> *gods, you will most certainly die. You won't last long in the land that you are crossing the Jordan to enter and possess. I call Heaven and Earth to witness against you today: I place before you Life and Death, Blessing and Curse. Choose life so that you and your children will live. And love God, your God, listening obediently to him, firmly embracing him. Oh yes, he is life itself, a long life settled on the soil that God, your God, promised to give your ancestors, Abraham, Isaac, and Jacob."*
>
> MSG

The path to true and abundant life is intricately tied to loving God, walking in His ways, and obeying His commandments. It's a call to embrace God's life-giving instructions and avoid the pitfalls that disobedience may lead to.

While some might perceive a catch, the choice is a testament to God's love and desire for our well-being. The passage urges us to choose life, love God obediently, and embrace the abundant life He promises. The Message version eloquently underscores the urgency of this decision, calling upon heaven and earth as witnesses.

Choosing a life aligned with God's commandments is not a burden but a pathway to true fulfillment. It shields us from troubles, leading us on a journey marked by His blessings. Falling in love with God makes His rules a joy to follow, creating a life rich in His promises and grace. As we count our blessings, may we also reflect on the choices that lead to a life filled with the abundance of God's love.

Chapter Thirty-Four

The Road to Colorado

In 2018, life threw me a curveball I never saw coming. I was laid off from my job at a local bank where I had been working for ten years. To make matters even more complicated, three other banks in the area were closing too, which meant the job market was saturated. As I sat there, staring at my empty calendar and wondering what to do next, I did the only thing that made sense—I prayed.

In the quiet of my heart, God whispered something that sounded more like a wild idea than divine direction: "Go to Colorado to Bible School."

Colorado? Bible School? At first, I thought, "That's crazy!" I had never even been to Colorado. But the more I prayed about it, the more peace settled over me, like a soft blanket of reassurance. Before I knew it, I was facing a tight deadline—just one month to apply and prepare to leave for their winter term. Amazingly, I was accepted. So,

I packed up my old GMC Yukon and set my sights westward, leaving North Carolina behind.

I didn't go into this adventure entirely alone. My cousin Vann, who clearly holds the title of "Best Cousin Ever," offered to ride with me and then fly back home. I was beyond grateful. Not just for the company, but because as soon as we hit Kentucky, my trusty Yukon decided it had had enough and broke down. This was the day before Thanksgiving, and as you can imagine, most places were closing for the holiday.

By God's grace, we managed to get a tow truck to a mechanic recommended by the driver. But the mechanic couldn't even look at the truck until after Thanksgiving. So, there we were, stranded with a small U-Haul trailer packed with all my belongings—furniture, kitchen stuff, bathroom essentials, everything. We had no choice but to leave the truck and the trailer in Kentucky.

Determined not to miss orientation, Vann and I rented a car and drove the rest of the way. Thanksgiving dinner? A gourmet feast of Burger King on the road. We arrived in Colorado late Thanksgiving night, exhausted but relieved.

Now, here's where God's favor shines through like a beacon. My childhood friend Kimie, who had recently moved to Colorado, had picked up the key to my new apartment—an apartment I secured over the phone without ever seeing it. When we walked in, I was overwhelmed with gratitude. Kimie had thoughtfully set up two air mattresses, complete with sheets, blankets, pillows, and even some towels. It felt like a warm hug from God Himself.

After a few days of settling in and picking up some temporary essentials like paper plates and plastic cutlery, Vann had to head back home. He drove to Denver, returned the rental car, and flew back to North Carolina. That left me in a new town with no car, most of my belongings still in Kentucky, and just a suitcase with some clothes I had managed to grab.

But Vann wasn't done being a hero. The very next week, he went back to Kentucky, picked up my truck and U-Haul, and drove them all the way to Colorado. If that isn't the favor of God, I don't know what is.

Looking back, every twist and turn, every breakdown and detour, was stitched together with threads of grace, provision, and divine favor. God had a plan all along, and it was more than I could have ever imagined.

Life Insight: Provision in Every Mile

Sometimes God's plans look nothing like ours. They come wrapped in uncertainty. They arrive through discomfort. They show up as detours we never wanted. But here's the truth I've learned: Obedience is not about having every answer. It is about trusting the One who already does.

Even when things fall apart, God is at work. He is moving pieces into place. He is aligning people, opportunities, and provision—right on time. The favor of God is not seen in a life free of struggle. It is seen in His faithfulness through the struggle.

God often calls you to step out when the road ahead is unclear. That is where faith grows. That is where you learn to lean on His wisdom instead of your own.

Proverbs 3:5-6 makes this clear:

> *"Trust in the Lord with all your heart and lean not on your own understanding; in all your ways submit to him, and he will make your paths straight."*
>
> NIV

This verse became real in my own story. Every obstacle turned into a stepping stone. Each challenge directed me closer to His purpose.

Romans 8:28 gives us the same promise:

> *"And we know that in all things God works for the good of those who love him, who have been called according to his purpose."*
>
> NIV

That means even breakdowns, delays, and disappointments have value. God weaves them into something far greater than what you see in the moment. What looks like a setback is often a setup for growth.

The lesson? Trust Him wholeheartedly—even when life looks nothing like you planned. His plans are always for your good. And always for His glory.

Chapter Thirty-Five

When Autocorrect Gets Spiritual

During my time in Colorado at Bible School, I had the honor of working for the founder and his ministry. I was part of his conference and event team, which meant I got to travel a few times a year to different states, helping coordinate teaching conferences held at hotels. My job was to plan the event, contract the hotels, and be on-site to ensure everything ran smoothly. As the event team manager, it was my responsibility to make sure things went off without a hitch.

Part of my role also involved working closely with the minister's security team—a dedicated group of men whose sole job was to ensure my boss was cared for and protected. These men were great—solid, dependable, and very straightforward, mostly from police and military backgrounds. I would occasionally text them with updates, using a no-nonsense style to match the tone of our work. Messages like, "Security Team: give me an ETA of arrival in the ballroom," or "Security Team: dinner will be served at this time..." were typical.

But then there was Arizona.

We were fresh out of COVID lockdowns, still navigating the maze of social distancing, temperature checks, and all the exhausting protocols that came with it. Long days blurred into even longer nights. In the middle of this whirlwind, I needed to send a quick update to the security team. Typing fast, mind racing with a million details, I shot off a message without double-checking it.

"Sexy Team: give me an ETA of arrival in the ballroom."

I hit send, glanced at the message, and froze. My eyes widened as the realization hit me. *Sexy Team?!* My face turned beat red, and then, unable to contain it, I burst out laughing—the kind of laugh that bubbles up from sheer exhaustion and disbelief. Here I was, the event team manager, accidentally labeling a group of retired police officers and military men, who worked for a *ministry*, as "sexy."

Thankfully, they had a great sense of humor. They teased me about it for months afterward, turning my mortifying moment into an inside joke that broke the tension whenever things got stressful. To this day, I cannot send a text without double-checking... and maybe chuckling a little at the memory.

Life Insight: Faith Beyond Comfort Zones

At one of our events in Orlando, our minister opened up an altar call for prayer for healing. The lines stretched endlessly, and though we had prayer ministers who were ministry partners and students from the Bible college, the need was overwhelming. We started calling on anyone from the event team to help pray with the congregation.

I had been trained at school to be on the prayer line, but I had never actually done it. Still, seeing the immense need, I jumped in. As I walked to the front of the congregation to line up with the prayer team, I prayed, "Lord, please let it be something simple, like a headache or something." But when the next people came up to me, it was a couple with their son in a wheelchair.

I thought to myself, *Really, God? This is what you bring to me? I can't heal this kid in a wheelchair!* But then I heard God speak clearly to my heart: *You can't heal anyone. I am the Healer; you are the conduit.*

In that moment, I realized it takes the same faith to pray for someone with a headache as it does for someone in a wheelchair. Was the child healed? Not instantaneously. But I know that my God is the Healer, and I believe in my heart that boy is healed.

The lesson? It is not about us. It never was. We are simply vessels. The power is God's, and our job is to trust, obey, and step out in faith—whether we are sending a text to the "Sexy Team" or praying for a miracle. And remember:

"I am the Lord who heals you."

Exodus 15:26, NIV

Chapter Thirty-Six

Enjoying the Pura Vida in Costa Rica

In my second year at Charis Bible College, I was thrilled to embark on our mandatory mission trip to Costa Rica. The week leading up to it was a whirlwind—first, a conference in Orlando with the ministry I was working for, and then straight to my mission trip. Thanks to some strategic luggage maneuvering, I managed to juggle both trips without a hitch.

After my Orlando adventure, I returned to Colorado to regroup with my classmates before jetting off to San Jose. Two others on my mission team were with me in Orlando, and since we had to get up so early for our flight and were not meeting our team until a very late flight, we went to a hotel to rest for a while. Before we knew it, we went back to the airport to catch our next flight. After a long day, we were finally on our way.

Once we arrived in San Jose, we passed through customs, met our guide and host, and boarded a bus to our hotel. Soon, we were settled, dining together, and sketching out our mission plan for the next 10 days: half in bustling San Jose and the other half in coastal Limon.

Months of preparation paid off as we hit the streets of San Jose armed with skits, dances, and powerful testimonies. Stepping out of our comfort zones was exhilarating, especially when strangers joined in the fun or stopped to listen to our message of love. But my favorite thing was the "Abrazos Gratis". Holding up signs saying "Abrazos Gratis" (Free Hugs) brought a range of reactions, from laughter to tears, but each embrace was a chance to share the love of Jesus tangibly. One lady laughed and said, "Only Americans would be crazy enough to give out free hugs." Yes, we were! But my favorites were the ones who were a little hesitant but would pull back from the hugs with tears in their eyes. I couldn't help but wonder how long it had been since someone had loved them. These were the ones I would pull back in, hug again, and tell them how much Jesus loved them!

Our days were a blur of ministry and fellowship, from block parties to heartfelt church services. Then came the journey to Limon, where the anticipation of jungle adventures and sloth sightings ran high. Our quaint bungalow-style hotel provided the base for our activities, including working with local kids, sharing messages of hope, and even squeezing in a visit to a sloth sanctuary.

As our time in Costa Rica came to an end, I couldn't help but reflect on its impact on me. Mission trips are not just about serving others—they're also about personal growth and connection. These memories of Costa Rica will stay with me forever, a reminder of the beauty of serving others and embracing the Pura Vida spirit.

Life Insight: Being the Hands and Feet of Jesus

In our journey of being Jesus's hands and feet, there are moments that stand out as profound reminders of the transformative power of love. One such moment occurred during a mission trip to Costa Rica, where our team embarked on a unique ministry endeavor—giving free hugs.

As we stood on the streets of San Juan holding up signs that read "Abrazos Gratis" (Free Hugs), we encountered a diverse array of reactions. Some people approached us with skepticism, unsure of our intentions. Others simply smiled and walked by, while a few laughed or shook their heads in disbelief.

But amidst the varied responses, there were those whose reactions touched our hearts deeply. Some individuals hesitantly approached us, their eyes betraying a sense of longing and loneliness. As we warmly embraced them, they would initially pull away, their eyes welling up with tears. In those tender moments, it became clear that these individuals had not experienced the love and comfort of human touch in a long time. They were hungry for connection, for acceptance, for love. In those tearful embraces, we saw the profound impact of sharing the love of Christ in tangible ways.

It wasn't just about the physical act of giving hugs but about extending Jesus's love and compassion to those who needed it most. It was about being vessels of His grace, mercy, and unconditional love. The importance of sharing the love of Christ cannot be overstated. In a world often filled with pain, brokenness, and division, love has the power to heal, restore, and unite.

As followers of Jesus, we are called to embody this love in everything we do, our words, actions, and interactions with others. In John 13:34, Jesus gives us a clear command:

> *"Love one another. As I have loved you, so you must love one another."*
>
> NIV

This is not merely a suggestion but a mandate for all who profess to follow Christ. We are called to love sacrificially, selflessly, and extravagantly, just as Jesus loved us. As I reflect on my experiences in Costa Rica and the profound impact of giving free hugs, I will be inspired to continue sharing the love of Christ wherever I go. May I be a vessel of His love, bringing healing, hope, and wholeness to a world desperate for God's love's transformative power.

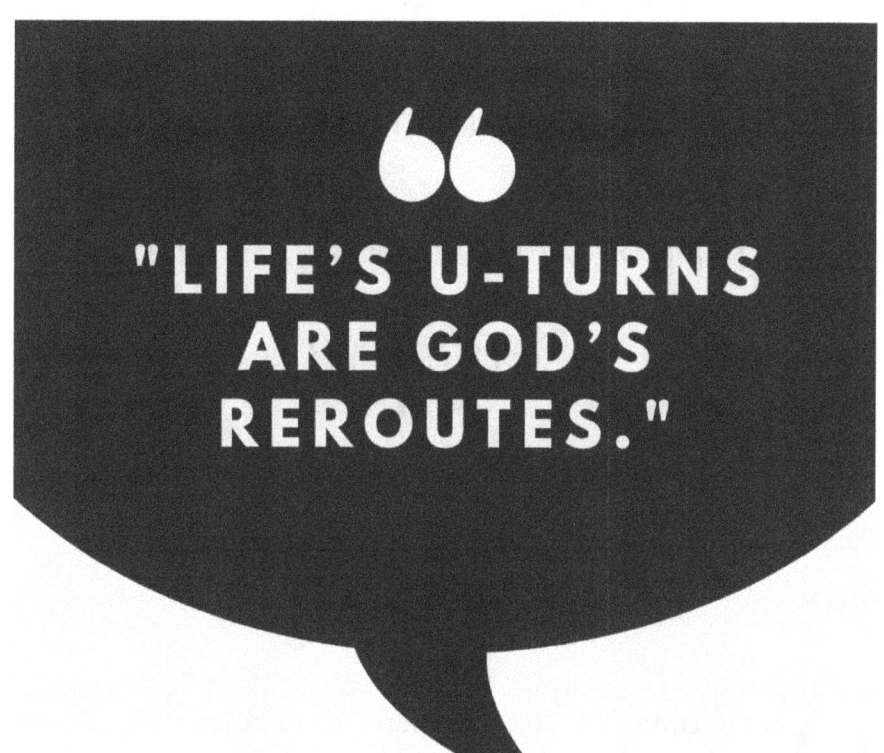

"LIFE'S U-TURNS ARE GOD'S REROUTES."

Chapter Thirty-Seven

Grief, Fur, and a New Beginning

On December 24, 2022, I experienced a heartbreak I wasn't ready for—my mom passed away. Her absence left a deep ache in my soul, and the weight of grief settled over me like a heavy fog. I was devastated. Life felt dim, and joy seemed like a memory from long ago.

In the midst of my depression, I heard something that stuck with me: "If you're struggling with sadness, get a dog." It sounded a little crazy at the time—impulsive even—but I was desperate for something, anything, that could help lift the heaviness. And so, by the end of January, I did something bold.

I bought a dog.

Growing up, I hadn't had a dog since I was a little girl, but I'd always dreamed of owning a Bernese Mountain Dog—those big, beautiful, gentle giants. The only thing that held me back was the shedding (and a little common sense). That's when I discovered the Bernedoodle—a crossbreed that offers the same sweet temperament with less of the mess. I found a breeder in Pennsylvania—an Amish family who only used their cell phone off-property, strictly for business. I left a message, she called me back, and I sent in my deposit.

Two weeks later, I loaded up the car with Melanie and my nephew Conner, and we hit the road from North Carolina to Pennsylvania. We left late on a Friday afternoon and drove nine hours straight. Somewhere along the way, we realized something surprising—we were heading back to the same small town where we'd visited an Amish farm during our legendary "No Parents Tour." Isn't it funny how God weaves stories together?

We stayed the night at a lovely hotel and resort in Bird-in-Hand, PA, and the next morning, we enjoyed the best breakfast before heading to the farm. It was snowing, such a peaceful, quiet snowfall, like God's hush over the land. When we arrived, the breeder had two male puppies left. I sat on the floor to meet them, and one little guy crawled into my lap, laid his head down, and let out a tiny sigh. That was it. He had chosen me.

We packed up my new 15-pound, 8-week-old baby, and he snuggled in my lap, shaking from fear and unsure of the world. We stopped at an outdoor store my nephew had followed online (coincidentally located in the same town), and I carried the puppy inside. Strangers immediately gathered around us, all gushing over the bundle of fluff in my arms. It felt like joy was waking up again.

As we headed home, we had a wild idea to take a scenic detour through Washington, D.C. We didn't get out of the car, because traffic was awful and patience was thin, especially with a crying puppy in the backseat. Eventually, we made it back to the highway, and after six more hours, several pit stops, and a few puppy meltdowns, we made it home.

I'll be honest—raising a puppy is no joke. There were (and still are) moments when I've thought, "What did I get myself into?" But nearly three years later, that scared little puppy is now a 105-pound gentle giant. He's the joy of my life. He fills the empty spaces with unconditional love, comic relief, and companionship I didn't even know I needed. He's been a balm to my broken heart—proof that sometimes healing doesn't come the way we expect.

Life Insight: When Joy Returns with Paws and a Tail

"So with you: Now is your time of grief, but I will see you again and you will rejoice, and no one will take away your joy."

John 16:22, NIV

Grief has a way of shrinking your world.

The colors fade. The laughter dulls. It's like someone pressed pause on your spirit, and everything stands still—except the ache. Even your prayers feel quieter, like whispers into the wind. Life keeps going around you, but your heart feels parked in the slow lane, unsure if it will ever catch up again.

I've been there. Maybe you have too.

But here's what I've learned in that stillness: **God is not absent in grief. He is near.** And while grief may knock the breath out of you, God is the One who sits quietly beside you—never rushing the process, never demanding a smile, just *being there*.

Sometimes, He brings comfort through scripture. Sometimes, through people. And sometimes? He brings it in the most unexpected form—like fur, floppy ears, and a tail that thumps a steady rhythm of hope.

I never expected healing to come wrapped in a puppy. But there he was—wide-eyed, wiggly, and somehow perfectly timed by Heaven. The first time he crawled into my lap and rested his tiny head on me, I felt something shift. Not a miracle cure. Not the erasing of sorrow. But a spark.

A quiet reminder that **joy and grief can coexist.**

Joy doesn't cancel out sorrow, but it *does* soften its edges. It adds color back into the world, little by little. It arrives in licks and snuggles and 3 a.m. potty breaks that somehow feel sacred because they remind you that you're still here. And life is still worth showing up for.

Grief teaches us many things, but one of its most humbling lessons is that **healing comes in layers.** It's not linear. It's not tidy. But it *is* holy.

God didn't remove my pain—but He *entered into it.* Just like that puppy climbed into my lap, God drew close. Not to fix everything right away, but to simply stay. To remind me I was not forgotten. Not alone. Not finished.

And now, years later, that once-tiny source of joy takes up half my bed, snores louder than a grown man, and follows me from room to room like I hung the moon. He's not just a dog—he's a reminder of God's promise: *I will see you again, and you will rejoice.*

Grief visited. But it didn't get to stay.

The sorrow came... but so did the Savior.
And joy followed close behind—on four furry legs.

Chapter Thirty-Eight

The Road to Rushmore: A Healing Trip West

After my mom passed away, just days before Christmas, our world cracked wide open. She and Dad had been together for 56 years—an entire lifetime of shared coffee cups, inside jokes, and side-by-side quiet moments. Watching my dad grieve her absence was heart-wrenching. He moved through the days like a man who had forgotten how to breathe. So when he mentioned that he had always wanted to see South Dakota—Mt. Rushmore and the wild, dusty streets of Deadwood—it felt like a divine invitation.

Two of my nephews and I hatched a plan: we'd take him west. Not just a vacation, but a road trip—a pilgrimage of sorts, for healing and remembering and making new memories in the wide, open spaces of America.

Dad hates flying, always has. So we packed the car in North Carolina and set out across the country—just us, the open road, and a cooler full of snacks. The drive was long. Really long. Somewhere around mile 1,200, we started wondering what we'd gotten ourselves into. But between the gas station laughs, singing along to classic country, and even a few "Are we there yet?" groans, something gentle was happening in the car. We were beginning to smile again.

When we finally arrived in South Dakota, it felt like stepping into a Western Dad had watched a hundred times. The land was rugged, and the air felt cleaner—like it had been waiting just for us. I had found us a house on Airbnb so we could each have our own room, a little space to breathe and unwind. As a bonus, it had a pool table in the basement, which quickly became our favorite evening pastime. Most nights you'd find us down there, cue sticks in hand, laughing, talking smack, and letting joy sneak back in through the cracks.

Mt. Rushmore was as majestic as he'd imagined. Dad stood quietly, eyes shining, staring up at those giant faces carved into stone, maybe thinking about all the years he and Mom had dreamed of seeing them together.

But it was Deadwood that really lit him up. The town still buzzes with the ghosts of gunslingers and gamblers, and Dad, a die-hard Western fan, was in his element. We watched as he wandered wide-eyed through the old saloons and wooden sidewalks, stopping to take photos and share stories about the outlaws he'd watched in film while growing up.

Then came the reenactment of Wild Bill Hickok's death. We were just watching from the crowd when one of the actors picked Dad to help with the scene. I'll never forget the grin that spread across his face—equal parts shy and thrilled. He played along like a pro, laughing and leaning into the moment. For those few minutes, he wasn't a grieving husband—he was just a man having a ball. Watching him, I felt my heart do something it hadn't done in a while: it soared.

We saw all the sights—Crazy Horse, Badlands, Custer State Park—but it was the moments in between that mattered most. Sitting around a table with my nephews and Dad, telling stories, remembering Mom, and quietly making space for new joy in our lives. The laughter didn't erase the grief, but it softened it. It reminded us that life still had goodness to offer.

The trip was bittersweet. Our first big memory without her. But it was also a beginning. A reminder that even in the shadow of loss, there is room for laughter, adventure, and healing.

We came back home with tired feet, full hearts, and a sense that maybe—just maybe—we were going to be okay.

Live Insight: God of the Long Road

Grief does not come with a map—no tidy set of directions to navigate the aching emptiness left behind. But sometimes, healing finds us in the most unexpected places: in the hum of tires on a long road trip, the crackle of a campfire shared with people who carry the same loss, and in the unmistakable sparkle in your dad's eyes as he plays along in a Wild West reenactment.

After loss, we often wonder if joy will ever dare to knock on our door again. The weight of sorrow can feel so heavy that laughter seems like a foreign language. But God, in His tender kindness, meets us right there in the middle of our sorrow. He does not rush us through it. Instead, He gently guides us to places where memories can be both honored and made new—where grief and joy are allowed to sit side by side.

That trip to South Dakota was never just about checking landmarks off a list. It was about seeing each other again—really seeing. It was about remembering that life, even after profound loss, still holds stunning beauty, unexpected surprises, and special moments that pull a laugh from deep inside you.

Grief did not vanish on that trip. It sat quietly with us. But so did joy. And in that tender space between the two, God breathed His comfort.

> *"You will show me the path of life; in Your presence is fullness of joy; at Your right hand are pleasures forevermore."*
> Psalm 16:11, NKJV

Chapter Thirty-Nine

Waves of Grief, Currents of Grace

Losing my mom on Christmas Eve 2022 was the worst time of my life. She was my best friend, my confidante, the person who always knew how to make everything better. Without her, I felt completely lost. Grief became my constant companion, shadowing even the moments that were supposed to be filled with joy.

June came, marking my 50th birthday—a milestone my mom would have celebrated with grandeur. She loved throwing parties, making every special occasion feel like an unforgettable event. I knew if she had been here, it would have been a big bash, filled with laughter, decorations, and her signature touch that made everyone feel cherished. Instead, it was a miserable day, heavy with her absence.

Then in August, my cousin talked me into going on a cruise with her and her parents. Coincidentally, the cruise fell on the week of my mom's birthday. I was hesitant. I did not want to go, but my cousin's persistence wore me down. I finally agreed, with one condition: I was going to focus on relaxing and allowing myself to work through my grief in my own way. I told her that if I did not feel up to doing something, I simply would not. I had no plans to get off the ship in Nassau. To my relief, she agreed. This trip was not about cramming in activities or chasing every excursion; it was about rest and reflection.

And that is exactly what it became. I had never stayed on the ship while at port before, but it turned out to be exactly what I needed. We lounged by the pool, basking in the sun without any rush or schedule. It was peaceful, almost therapeutic. The ship was quiet with most passengers off exploring, leaving us with a serene, almost sacred space to just be.

We did decide to get off at the private island, though—I simply could not resist the allure of that clear blue water. We rented a cabana for the first time, and it was wonderful. Having our own little oasis, complete with a fan to keep us cool, felt like a luxury I did not know I needed. Floating in the cove, I felt a rare sense of calm wash over me. I could not help but think of my mom. She loved floating in the ocean, the gentle rocking of the waves always bringing her joy. In that moment, I felt close to her, as if the water carried whispers of her laughter.

On the night of my mom's birthday, I found myself drawn to the ship's casino. Memories flooded back of our first cruise together, where she discovered the roulette table and laughed like a kid at Christmas. She thought it was the most fun, giggling with every spin, her joy infectious. In her honor, I decided to play. I do not believe in luck, and I do not think of her in heaven pulling strings to tip the odds in my favor. But that night, I won over $600 at that roulette table.

I will call it the favor of God. Not because He endorses gambling, but because He loves me. In His tender, compassionate way, I believe He just wanted me to smile, to feel a spark of joy on a day that could have been swallowed by sadness. That win was not about the money; it was a reminder that even in grief, even in the absence of the ones we love most, there are moments of light, moments of grace. And in those moments, I carry my mom with me, her laughter echoing in my heart.

Life Insight: The Sacred Pause - Resting in God

Grief has a way of making us feel like life should stop—yet somehow, the world keeps spinning. The dishes still pile up. The bills still come. The clock keeps ticking as if the universe missed the memo that your heart is shattered.

In these moments, the **sacred pause** becomes not only important but *essential*. Grief is not a mountain to conquer or a puzzle to solve. It is a tender path, one we must walk slowly, with reverence for both the loss and the love that lingers.

In Psalm 46:10, God says,

"Be still, and know that I am God."

NIV

This is more than an invitation—it is a lifeline. To *be still* is not to do nothing. It is to stop striving. To loosen your grip on trying to control what you cannot. To rest in the holy assurance that even when your world is falling apart, **God is holding it—and you—together.**

Let us be honest: in grief, everything feels undone. Your emotions may swing wildly from numbness to tears to anger to exhaustion. The temptation is to busy yourself, to scroll endlessly, to stay occupied so you do not have to *feel*. But hear this, dear friend: **you do not need to outrun your grief. You are allowed to rest in it.**

Rest is not weakness. It is an act of *trust*.
It is a declaration that says: *"I do not have to hold it all together. God is already doing that for me."*

Psalm 34:18 whispers this comfort:

> *"The Lord is close to the brokenhearted and saves those who are crushed in spirit."*

NIV

Notice—He is not standing at a distance, waiting for you to pull yourself together. He is near. He is saving. He is cradling your crushed spirit with His tenderness.

So, beloved, **give yourself permission to pause.**
Let the tears fall—they are not a sign of failure but of love.
Sit in the quiet—not because you have all the answers, but because **the God of all comfort is present in the stillness.**

And when the ache feels unrelenting, remember this: *Even when you cannot feel Him, even when your prayers are groans instead of words—God is holding you. He is whispering hope into the deepest, most fragile parts of your soul.*

Rest here. Breathe here. Grieve here. And in this sacred pause, trust that **healing begins—not in rushing ahead, but in resting with the One who never lets you go.**

Chapter Forty

The People Who Shape Us

Of all the incredible things I have experienced in my travels, it is the people who stand out the most. From the indifferent French and reserved Germans to the warm-hearted Scots we met in Switzerland, the loving Mexicans, and the beautiful Haitians—each person left a mark on me in some way.

I know many who believe travel is a waste of money, arguing that it leaves nothing tangible behind. But to me, travel is something entirely different. Everywhere I go, I bring a piece of it home—not in the form of a tacky souvenir, but in the lessons it teaches me.

In Mexico, I learned that I can accomplish anything if I set my mind to it. In London, I discovered what true friendship looks like. In Haiti, I experienced unconditional love, and on a trip to Maine, I finally listened to what my heart had been telling me all along. These lessons are priceless—things no sale item could ever compare to.

I also hope that, in some small way, I have left an impact on the people I have met. Perhaps a word of encouragement or a simple act of kindness gave someone a moment they will cherish forever.

Mission trips have been some of the most life-changing experiences of my journey. Many critics dismiss them as glorified vacations, but you would be surprised by what can happen in just a week. Not only do you realize how incredibly blessed we are, but you also begin to feel the compassion Jesus had when He looked upon the multitudes.

I will never forget my first trip to Haiti when I truly understood what it meant to empathize with Jesus. I remember trying to find a quiet place to pray or read, only to be surrounded by people—wanting to sit with me, touch me, or simply watch me. Even a simple walk meant having a crowd of at least twenty people following us.

For the first time, I could imagine what Jesus must have felt—constantly surrounded by those in need, reaching out in hope that He would see their pain and do something about it. At the end of each day, my sandaled feet were covered in dust and grime, and I finally understood why foot-washing was such a meaningful act in biblical times.

That week, I walked in Jesus' sandals. I saw immense need and felt the weight of knowing that while I could feed a starving child for the time I was there, I could not stop wondering—what would happen after I left?

So, what difference does a week in the mission field make? It opens eyes and hearts. It gives us stories to share, stirring others to give, pray, or even go themselves. It allows us to stand in the gap for those too weary to stand on their own. It reminds us to support those who have dedicated their lives to serving—whether in Haiti, Mexico, Africa, or even in our own neighborhoods.

Because while the gospel is free, it takes resources to spread it. And when the Lord asks, "Whom shall I send?" we can boldly answer, **"Here am I, Lord, send me"** (Isaiah 6:8).

Life Insight: I Love You

Before stepping into ministry, an uncle of mine—who has since gone on to be with the Lord—gave me a piece of advice I will never forget. He said, *"The one thing you need to do is minister love."*

In a world filled with counterfeit love, people are desperately searching for something real. And the truth is, only God's love satisfies. It is not the love of family, friends, or a significant other that fills the deepest void—it is **agape** love, the unconditional love of God.

Agape love is steadfast, unshaken by circumstances. Before you even existed, God loved you so much that He gave His Son to redeem and set you free. **He is love.** As 1 John 4:7-8 says:

"Beloved, let us love one another, for love is of God, and everyone who loveth is born of God and knoweth God. He that loveth not knoweth not God, for God is love."

KJV

As believers, we are called to reflect that love. But let's be honest—love is not always easy. When we are hurt or offended, our natural response is not to love but to retaliate. Yet Jesus calls us to a different standard. He told us to forgive *seventy times seven* (Matthew 18:22) and to love our neighbors as ourselves (Matthew 22:39). Imagine the difference that kind of love could make in the world!

One of the most powerful examples of love in action is found in the Garden of Gethsemane. When soldiers came to arrest Jesus, Peter—acting in defense—drew his sword and cut off a soldier's ear. But instead of responding with anger, Jesus did something remarkable. He told Peter to put away his sword, then reached down, picked up the ear, and miraculously restored it (Luke 22:50-51).

That is love.

Jesus endured torture, bore our sin, and even spent three days in hell so we would never have to. **That** is the greatest love—laying down one's life for another (John 15:13).

So, as you go about your day, remember: **you are the hands and feet of Jesus.**

You may encounter people who are rude, indifferent, or vastly different from you. Love them anyway. Show them the heart of God, because the only way they may ever experience His love is through you.

Every person—red, yellow, black, brown, and white—is precious in His sight.

And they need to know.

TONYA KAY MCKINLEY

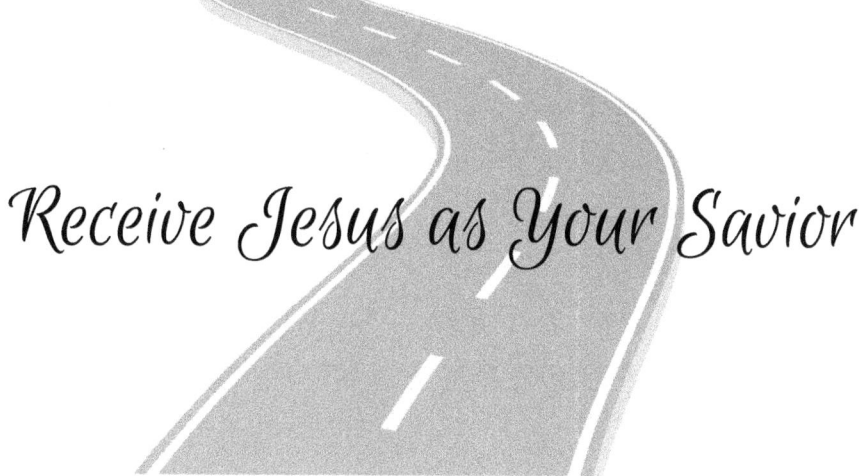

Receive Jesus as Your Savior

Dear Friend,

If you've reached this page, I believe it is no accident. God has been pursuing your heart since the moment you were formed in your mother's womb. His love for you is immeasurable, and His desire is for you to walk in the fullness of your identity as His beloved child.

This journey begins with one decision: accepting Jesus Christ as your Lord and Savior. Jesus came into this world, lived a sinless life, and gave His life on the cross to pay the penalty for our sins. But the story didn't end there. He rose from the grave, victorious over sin and death, so that you and I could have eternal life and a restored relationship with God.

Romans 10:9-10 tells us:
"If you declare with your mouth, 'Jesus is Lord,' and believe

> *in your heart that God raised him from the dead, you will be saved. For it is with your heart that you believe and are justified, and it is with your mouth that you profess your faith and are saved."*

Salvation is a gift, freely given by grace. You don't have to earn it, work for it, or clean yourself up before coming to Jesus. All He asks is for you to come as you are.

Would you like to take that step today?

Pray this prayer from your heart:

"Lord Jesus,
I come to You today, realizing that I am a sinner in need of a Savior. Thank You for loving me so much that You died for my sins and rose again to give me new life. I confess that You are Lord, and I believe that You were raised from the dead. Forgive me for my sins, and wash me clean. I surrender my life to You. Fill me with Your Holy Spirit and help me to walk in the fullness of my identity as a daughter of the King. Thank You for saving me. In Your precious name, Amen."

If you've prayed that prayer, welcome to the family of God! You are now a new creation in Christ (2 Corinthians 5:17), and heaven is rejoicing over you (Luke 15:7).

What's next?

1. **Talk to God daily.** Prayer is simply having a conversation with Him.

2. **Read the Bible.** Start with the Gospel of John to learn more about Jesus.

3. **Join a community of believers.** Find a church where you can grow and be encouraged.

4. **Share your story.** Let others know about the decision you've made today!

You are loved, cherished, and chosen.

With love and joy,
Tonya

About the Author

Tonya Kay McKinley is a passionate speaker, minister, and writer with a heart for empowering women to embrace their God-given identity. She holds a degree in Theology and has dedicated her life to helping others discover the transformative love of Christ.

Tonya makes her home in North Carolina, where she lives with her faithful and furry companion, Boulder. Whether she's walking scenic trail, studying scripture, or sharing her message at events, she brings warmth, humor, and authenticity to everything she does.

As the founder of Hadassah Ministries, Tonya equips women to walk boldly in their calling as daughters of the King. Through her writing, she invites readers to explore their faith, face life's challenges with a TIARA attitude, and find their unique place in God's Kingdom.

Other Works

"Stumbling Down the Road Less Traveled: A Devotional: Insights Into Life's Mishaps on the Road." Published February, 2008.

"Finding Your Love Story: Fall in Love with the One Who Loved Your First." Published August, 2021.

"Finding Your Love Story: A Bible Study: Fall in Love with the One Who Loved You First." Published August, 2021.

"A Princess Proclamation." Published January, 2024.

"A Prince's Pledge." Published January, 2024.

"Beloved: A Love Letter From God." Published March, 2025

www.hadassah-ministries.org & www.tonyakaymckinley.com

Scan the QR Codes for a direct link to my author website and to my ministry website.

A Final Word of Encouragement:
Beloved, never forget that you are seen, known, and deeply loved. Your life is a beautiful story still being written by the Author of love Himself. Lean into Him, trust His heart, and walk boldly in the truth that you are cherished beyond measure.

You are loved. You are chosen. You have a destiny.

www.ingramcontent.com/pod-product-compliance
Lightning Source LLC
Chambersburg PA
CBHW060151050426
42446CB00013B/2770